HERE'S TO THE FRIARS

The Heart of
Show Business

SOME *of* The **FRIARS** *in* The **FRIAR'S FROLIC, MAY, 1916**

Standing Left to Right – 1 *Andrew Mack* 2 *Neil O'Brien* 3 *Jas. J. Corbett* 4 *Harry Kelly* 5 *Felix Adler*
6 *Harlan Dixon* 7 *Geo. Daugherty* 8 *Vaughn Comfort* 9 *Johnny King* 10 *Tom Dingle* 11 *Eddie Garvey*
12 *Julius Tannen* 13 *Geo. Sidney* 14 *Tommy Gray* 15 *Bert Levy*

Seated Left to Right – 1 *Max Figman* 2 *Laddie Cliff* 3 *Will Rogers* 4 *Sam Harris* 5 *Jerry J. Cohan*
6 *Louis Mann* 7 *Fred Niblo* 8 *Geo. M. Cohan* 9 *Lew Dockstader* 10 *Frank Tinney*

The old 56th Street Monastery.   *The present Monastery at 57 East 55th Street.*

HERE'S TO THE FRIARS

The Heart of Show Business

by
JOEY ADAMS

Crown Publishers, Inc.
New York

Inquiries should be addressed to Crown Publishers, Inc., One Park Avenue, New York, N.Y. 10016.

Published simultaneously in Canada by
General Publishing Company Limited

Printed in the United States of America

Library of Congress Cataloging in Publication Data

Adams, Joey, 1911-
    Here's to the Friars.

    1. Friars Clubs, New York. 2. Entertainers—United States—Interviews. I. Title.
PN1572.F73A3   1976   791'.06'57471   76-18995
ISBN 0-517-52788-X

Contents

Saluting Frank Sinatra at Friars roast, February 24, 1976. Frank Jr., Mayor Abe Beame, and Governor Hugh Carey at the Waldorf-Astoria.

1

The Roasting of Sinatra

Uncle Miltie said to Sinatra: "If your zipper could only talk!"

Don Rickles remarked: "Don't just sit there, Frank—enjoy yourself —hit somebody!"

Howard Cosell purred: "Sinatra is an antique relic of yesteryear— he is the Paul Anka of the menopause set!"

It was the annual Friars roast and fund raiser. It was in honor of Frank Sinatra and it was the most expensive in history. Five hundred dollars for the first-class seats and $200 per in the economy section. Two hundred seventy-five thousand dollars was raised and over a thousand humans came out of their homes from all over the world not to praise the emperor but to bury him.

That's the way it is with the world famous theatrical club, the Friars. They do you in to do you proud.

And why Frank Sinatra? Because he's the biggest and the best. Because he'll flush out the biggest names and the best spenders. Because he'll fill the room and sell the journal. Because that's the way the game is played.

And why not, you ask, the cute freckle-faced redhead on your favorite TV serial? Why don't they honor him? or her? or it? Because who cares about him or her or it? Nobody except maybe his mother, his agent, or his creditors. Okay, so the freckle-faced kid is nice to his mother. Okay, so he doesn't smoke—not even pot—but so what?

So Sinatra is a little temperamental. So he flattened a few critics. So he declared war on Australia. It reminds me of the time I was on the set with Marilyn Monroe. She was always late and invariably blew her lines. I asked Billy Wilder, the director, how he could take her temperament. Billy said: "I have an Aunt Sylvia in Cleveland.

She's always on time, makes a wonderful chicken soup, never forgets your birthday—but who would come to see her?"

So that's why it's Sinatra. Like it's been for Bob Hope, Jack Benny, Desi and Lucy, Martin and Lewis, Barbra Streisand, Tom Jones, George M. Cohan, and so many others over the years. Every year another dinner. Every year another guest of honor. Every year another amount raised for the Friars charities.

Sinatra dredged out Cary Grant, Milton Berle, Georgie Jessel, Robert Merrill, Jan Murray, Don Rickles, Mayor Abe Beame, Governor Hugh Carey, Spiro Agnew, Sarah Vaughan, Ed McMahon, John Denver, Frank Sinatra, Jr., and a ton and a half of other celebrities stamped U.S. Prime.

Milton Berle summed it up: "We are all here for one reason and one reason only. You can sum it up in one word: *fear!*"

Jan Murray said: "Invitations were extended to this dinner for Frank in an unusual fashion. A guy drove up in a cement truck and asked me for my shoe size."

Berle noted: "What a crowd! I would say mob—but you know how sensitive Frank is.

"This aging Jerry Vale is very charitable. He built the Eisenhower Hospital in Palm Springs—and put all his friends in it."

Georgie Jessel talked for himself and George Burns: "I'm sorry Burns couldn't be here but something came up—and he was very proud." George praised Frank Sinatra, Jr.'s, singing. When he was told that Junior was twenty-nine years old he remarked, "I've got underwear older than that."

Comedian Pat Henry took note of the $500-a-plate charge and said he'd ask for a doggy bag to take home leftovers. "But I'm not walking through my neighborhood with $400 worth of meat."

Pat praised his idol as a family man: "And he thinks of the press as family. How often I have heard Sinatra say to Jilly Rizzo, 'Get rid of these mothers.'"

Cary Grant said: "On my feet I cease to function. To tell the truth, I can't function when I'm lying down either—that's why I love your style, Frank."

"What's all the fuss about this elderly Bobby Vinton?" Howard Cosell wanted to know. "He's a grandfather. And the kid is just like him. The first photo made of the new grandchild—the kid slugged the photographer."

"I'll tell you one thing about Sinatra," Berle shouted, "no one has

Frank sings special lyrics to Sophie Tucker at the Friars X-rated luncheon in her honor —the first Friar so endowed.

The author teaches Frank his first bad habit.

ever been turned away from his door—*if*—you're over twenty-one and have big knockers." Milton added that Frank made it the hard way: "He came from a little town. The town was so small the local hooker was a virgin.

"Frank has never let anything put him down. Once he went to visit a little old man in a hospital in Hoboken and he sang to the poor soul for an hour. When he was finished he said to him: 'I hope you get better.' And the little old man said, 'You, too!'"

Of course, the two MC's didn't escape the scalpels, Ed McMahon and Howard Cosell, better known as Big Mac and Big Mouth. They were introduced by Dean Buddy Howe as "a couple of good eggs" and you know where eggs come from.

Pat Henry said: "Cosell does so many things—all of them badly. I finally figured out the reason for his success—he hasn't improved."

"McMahon has a lot of talent," Berle remarked, "but it's in Johnny Carson's name." Jessel said, "I don't know if you heard about it but Ed likes to take a drink once in a while. In fact, Carson didn't know he's a drinker until he came to work sober one night."

I don't know who said it. I think it was I: "Howard Cosell's show was canceled. The critics thought it was good, but word of mouth killed it."

Sinatra's generosity was emphasized. How he gives away a fortune. Once in Las Vegas Frank saw a bent-over old man emptying ashtrays in the casino and he threw him four $100 bills. The little old man said, "Keep your money, schmuck. I'm trying to clean up my hotel—I'm Howard Hughes."

Berle said: "Everything Sinatra touches turns to gold. I'm afraid to go to the toilet with him."

And he's a great philanthropist. When Eddie Fisher went bankrupt, Frank opened his wallet and showed him a picture of Gloria DeHaven.

Jan Murray: "Frank invited me to live here at the Waldorf with him. 'Live my life,' he said. My heart said yes but my prostate said no."

Ed McMahon said, "Frank speaks to God. Not in prayer but like on a one-to-one basis. Sinatra almost didn't make it here tonight. He was taking a walk and was hit by a motorboat."

Cosell introduced Don Rickles at the end of the show: "Normally we wouldn't give this part of the program to a rat. But we changed our mind—here is Don Rickles."

4

"I'll tell you how big Sinatra is," Don Rickles said, "he wears a cross in nobody's honor." Don said: "When you enter the room you have to kiss his ring. I don't mind—but he has it in his back pocket."

Robert Merrill sang: "When Frank sings Pagliacci, he sounds like Liberace."

Georgie Jessel compared his life to Arnold Palmer: "He's made a fortune out of his putts and mine has broken me completely."

Former Vice-President Spiro Agnew said: "I can neither roast nor praise Frank Sinatra. I can only tell you that this man brings new dimensions to the words friendship and loyalty—I am honored to be his friend."

Sinatra said it all: "I thank you all. You know, my father wasn't born in this country but I thank him for making sure that *I* was born in this blessed America.

"My fellow Friars and friends—Put me down for a favor. I owe each and every one of you one. I give you my marker."

2

The Monastery

In 1912 when George M. Cohan became the Abbot, he gave us the Benediction. He said: "The idea of the Friars Club is to boost and not to knock." Decades later at a Friars roast Johnny Carson upgraded this concept with: "We only roast those we love. Everything we say here tonight is strictly for laughs—we really love each other—and if you believe that I have some swampland in Jersey I'd like to unload on you."

George M. Cohan said: "I do not claim that Friars are ideal characters. If they were, they wouldn't be human. The main thing about a Friar is that he tries to do the right thing by his brother. The most we can accomplish in this world is to do the best we can for our fellowmen and this is the great big, live thing in the Friars Club— we are boosters, not knockers."

I suppose the boosting spirit came naturally because the club was founded by press agents. A press agent—that's a guy who makes you well known to a lot of people who don't particularly want to know you. A press agent defines one of the prime differences between an actor and a civilian. When a civilian's house burns down he calls his insurance agent; when an actor's house burns down he calls his press agent.

The Press Agents Association, out of which grew the Friars, was Scotch-taped together in the autumn of 1904. Its initial purpose was to put the finger on the "free press" frauds who persistently and cleverly managed to scrounge "complimentary" admission to New York theatres. In other words, it was death to the freebies. The first meeting at Browne's Chop House was called by Charles Emerson Cook, press rep for David Belasco, Channing Pollock, representing the Shuberts, and John Flaherty for the Majestic Theatre. They prepared a blacklist and the blackest of the list were smoked out, stamped out, and thrown out.

The Frier COMPLIMENTARY DINNER TO

1. George M. Cohan, 2. Enrico Caruso, 3. Victor Herbert, 4. Gatti-Casazza (Gen. M'G'R Met.), 5. Campanini (Met. Con'D'R), 6. Raymond Hitchcock, 7. Scotti (Met. Baritone), 8. Rennold Wolf, 9. Will Rogers, 10. Gus Van, 11. Joe Schenck, 12. Irving Berlin, 13. Marcus Loew, 14. E. Ray Goetz, 15. Chauncey Olcott, 16. Joseph E. Schenck, 17. Sam Harris, 18. ZIT, 19. Daniel Frohman, 20. Channing Pollock, 21. John Pollock, 22. Police Commissioner Daugherty, 23. Leo Carrillo, 24. Louis Mann, 25. Sam Shipman, 26. Jimmy Walker, 27. Jean Schwartz, 28. Will Morrisey, 29. Felix Adler, 30. Judge Walter C. Kelly, 31. Steve Reardon, 32. Bert Leslie, 33. Doc Amey, 34. Dr. Leo Michel, 35. Nate Spingold, 36. Edgar Allen Wolff, 37. Maurice Rose, 38. Maurice Abrahams, 39. Jack Curtis, 40. Harry Rapp, 41. Lew Golder, 42. Jess Dandy, 43. Mike Selwyn, 44. Henry Bergman, 45. Max Winslow, 46. Fred Block, 47. George Sidney, 48. Jack Gleason, 49. Louis Silvers, 50. Silvio Hein, 51. Oscar Figman, 52. Barry Saranoff

Come 1906 another call went out for another meeting of press agents. This one was staged at Keen's Chop House. The membership naturally broadened to include press agents throughout the country, which naturally widened to include their clients, who naturally were producers, theatre owners, and actors. The club started to take on a personality.

The press agents, ever itchy to find another way to scratch their clients' egos and always looking for a new promotional angle, came up with the idea of the guest-of-honor dinner. They kicked off a series of dinners to noted men, principally within the theatrical profession and principally their paid-up clients. This method of garnering publicity for their customers was coincidentally doing the same for their club. The first honoree was Clyde Fitch and the feed was at the Café des Beaux Arts. In the same year grapefruit, underdone chicken, and baked Alaska evenings were given to Marc Klaw, Henry Miller, Oscar Hammerstein, and Victor Herbert. It was at the Herbert dinner that the famous Friars song, with words by Charles Emerson Cook and music by Victor Herbert, burst upon us for the first time.

THE FRIARS SONG

The Friars of old were a merry old fold,
    Care and Sadness to them were but folly;
With pipe and with glass, and an eye for a lass,
    And a quip, to defy melancholy.
Well versed in the stars and in musical bars,
    Dispensers of fiction and fable;
And at friendship's command they would pass the
        glad hand
With a toast that would ring 'round the table.

CHORUS:

Here's to the Friars! Here's to them all!
Out on the road, or here in the hall.
Raise high your glasses with cheer that inspires!
    And drink a deep toast
    To the boys we love most
A toast to all other good Friars!

Now, on with your cowls! And away with your scowls!
  For good fellowship still shall reward us.
It's clear as can be, loyal Friars are we;
  Ev'ry man of us has taken orders.
So, true to the name, let us gladly proclaim
  Fraternity that wants no urger;
In this land of Good Cheer, with its brotherhood dear,
  We are one, with no need for a "merger."

To-night no stars shine, neither your star nor mine;
  So we'll sing, as we strike up the band, boys,
To ev'ry true chap on the breadth of the map,
  Out from here to the far one-night stand, boys.
Too oft we must prate others' virtues as great,
  In one well self-advertised pageant,
But to-night, with a will (while we O.K. the bill),
  Let us drink to the health of the agent.

CHORUS:

In June 1907 a constitution was adopted and the fraternal order of the brotherhood of drumbeaters banded together under the name of The Friars. Wells Hawks became its first abbot, Charles Emerson Cook its first dean. Meetings were at one time at the Café des Beaux Arts, another time at the Hotel Hermitage, and at this time the young Turks or old Presbyterians (or whoever the progressives were) felt that they needed a permanent home. Eventually the building at 107 West 45th Street was acquired, reconstructed, and on May 9, 1908, the Monastery formally opened free of debt.

And how did the Friars get their name? I tried to dig up some of the old members—and I'd really have to—to find out the true story. I ended up with so many answers I'm going to let you choose your own.

The press agents claim that they started it. Now press agents being a hungry breed, they invariably hung out in an eatery. At Keen's Chop House they were fed principally on fries. One day it would be fish fry, the next day clam fry, and so on. And always it would be seasoned with Worcestershire. One theory is that from this sauce the name of "fryers" was hung on them. This later assumed a different construction and spelling and evolved into the FRIARS.

JERRY COHAN   GEORGE M. COHAN

FRIARS ALL STAR
FROLIC 1916

Another angle is that to attract attention to their new clubhouse they needed a space-grabbing stunt. They decided to stage a parade. Off they trundled to a theatrical costumer. As the story goes, the only costumes available were monks' robes from a busted Broadway show and that's how they inherited the cognomen of Friars.

A sidewise view of that story was once told by William F. Harrover who, in 1907, was prop man for Charles Emerson Cook's operetta *The Rose of the Alhambra. Rose,* which folded fast, featured a monastery scene with a chorus and a tub of Friars' robes. Cook requisitioned the robes and instead of shipping them to the warehouse with the rest of the stuff, he sent them to Keen's Chop House, his new club's new home. Had *The Rose of the Alhambra* been SRO, the Friars' robes would have stayed with the show and who knows what the club would have been called.

Wagnalls and his pal Funk define *monastery* as a home for religious retirement for brothers of a certain order. That's the best clue of all. The Friars became a home where one religiously retires from wives, girl friends, and other members of the familias Bund. In a moment of deep prayerful revelation or in the afterglow of a good pastrami on rye, the original group felt the need of a slogan. Eagerly they sought the various tomes of learning. One of the press agents happened to have gone to school and he came up with the Latin motto *Omnia fraternas prae,* which pressed into a blender comes out something like "One for all and all for one." Somewhere along the line a little old Jewish plaque maker must have given it the Hebrew reading from right to left or something because it somehow changed to *Prae omnia fraternitas,* which really means "Before all things—brotherhood." Whichever way you slice it, it means all Friars are brothers and this same spirit has permeated the hallowed halls since the club was incorporated under the name of the National Association of the Friars.

The brothers played happily in their West 45th Street friary for eight years. On May 22, 1916, they opened a bigger and better Monastery at 106–108–110 West 48th Street at a cost of $426,228 —give or take a few cents. Abbot George M. Cohan personally christened the cornerstone on October 21, 1915, with a bottle of champagne. Furthermore, it was Abbot Cohan himself who started the Friars Frolics and benefit shows that helped hoist the mortgage.

The day the 48th Street clubhouse opened its doors it became

They're all laughing—the dinner was on the house. Seated left to right, *Eve Block, Ida Cantor, Eddie, Gracie Allen, Al Jolson.* Standing left to right, *Benny Fields, Blossom Seeley, Harry Ruby, George Burns, Gracie Fields, Jesse Block.*

the sanctuary for the people of show business. With their own theatre, billiard rooms, cardrooms, dining rooms, and upholstered corners for shoptalk, no monk ever had it so good. The first order of business was to change the constitution so as to make the club strictly theatrical. It was submitted to the members on March 19, 1917, and passed unanimously: "The retention of the theatrical character is absolutely essential for its perpetuation, therefore we decree that a majority of the governors shall be persons exclusively conducting business or executive departments of theatres, theatrical companies or other standard amusement enterprises or persons actively engaged in the theatrical business as press agents, actors, or instrumental artists, or acknowledged dramatic and other authors and composers."

It is this theatrical atmosphere that gives it value not only to those engaged in the business of show business but also to those who, not being in the profession, are sympathetically in touch with it. The Friars developed cachet. It became the status symbol for celebrities, the "in" place to be. When press agents hustled in their star clients it was the beginning of big time. Show-business personalities are like magnets. The bigger they are the bigger the names they attract.

Friar Sam H. Harris who producd memorable shows in partnership with George M. Cohan said it when he wrote the following story in the *Friars' Epistle*. He called it "Friarly Friendship":

> My best friends are Friars. The best times I've ever had with my best friends have been enjoyed in the Friars Club. It's just one of those associations which have become so dear to my heart that I now think of the Friars and all that goes with the word as something which is part of me. In a man's life I don't suppose there are formed more than a dozen friendships which are true enough to withstand any conceivable sling of fate. Surely there are no more than a few associations made in a man's career which can bring him great relief of mind in just the thought of them. A man's love of his church or the little red brick schoolhouse or his home or his college can

Ted Lewis's house—the Friars annex—with Joe E. Lewis, Sophie Tucker, and Ted Lewis.

be associations like this. I never had the opportunity to call any institution "Alma Mater." I know my friends won't think I'm "slopping over" when I say that my regard for the Friars is one of the dearest things in my life. Thinking of the Club is a solace to me. It's a place I can turn to when life gets a little complex, as it has a habit of doing, and I can be sure of relief with the boys. I've been with old graduates when their voices choked as they yodeled the words of their college tune. It's a grip like this that the Friars gets on my heart. It's understandable, after all. I guess it's sort of an alma mater for me, the old place on Forty-eighth Street.

Showmen like the Sam Harrises of the world attract newspapermen, society folk, and politicians who always flock to where the spotlight shines the brightest. Even Hizzoner the Mayor of the City of New York, the Right Honorable Jimmy Walker, joined "the old place on Forty-eighth Street." He took an ad in the *Friars' Epistle* saying: "The Chief Magistrate of the City of New York—the city we are all pleased to call the greatest in the world—is proud and happy in the knowledge that he is a Friar," and he signed it "Friar James J. Walker."

And what is a Friar? He is a press agent, an actor, a producer, a hoofer, a vaudevillian, a picture star. He's a theatrical agent, a songwriter, a promoter, a nightclub owner, a TV executive, a newspaperman who likes to be with his own, the people he writes about. Or he's a doctor, lawyer, Indian chief, or businessman who loves show people and show business.

To this day the membership is two-thirds professional and one-third civilian. The dues work similarly. Civilians pay about twice the initiation fee and yearly dues of the professionals, and they are happy to do it to rub shoulders with the glossiest names on this planet.

Forty-eighth Street became a wateringhole for the newspaper fraternity. Since a press agent is as helpless without a newspaperman as Abbott was without Costello, the gents from the press were invited in and allowed to pay for the privilege. They no sooner cadged their first drinks than the friendly rivalry began and the Friars from the Fourth Estate were divided on whether or not to let the press agents stay as members! Editor and columnist Jack Lait of the New York *Daily Mirror* cracked, "Just because they were the originals it does not follow at all that they must survive. The Indians first settled Manhattan Island but look at 'em now!"

The opening of the new clubhouse at 57 East 55th Street and at present. After parading through the streets and throwing the key away, denoting never to close; from left to right, Ray Bloch, Jack E. Leonard, Abbot Joe E., Dean Harry Delf, and Harry Winston.

Friar Sime Silverman, the editor and founder of *Variety*, buttressed his reason for membership thusly: "The Friars, from the newspapermen's viewpoint, has many virtues. At the club the homeward-bound reporter obtains his news notes for another day. For such a service the newspaperman in Hicksville has his Masonic, Elks, Lions, or Rotary clubs. The New York and Broadway reporter has his Friars Club.

"But for every bit of news he gathers, and for every moment of relaxation at the club, he pays and pays and pays. And the payoff is at home answering or dodging questions or both.

"With the grade of acid and reverse English that only a newspaperman's wife can get into such a question, the reporter's wife coyly asks, 'Did you get a lot of news while playing four spades doubled with a sore loser for a partner at the club last night?' Don't answer—just duck!"

The Friars were zonked with their first flop in 1932. The Depression took hold even though the 48th Street Monastery was ablaze

I Geo. M. Cohan	*March* 1920		XI Irving Berlin
II Jimmy Walker	V Daniel Frohman	VIII Sam Harris	XII Bugs Baer
III Willie Collier	VI David Belasco	IX Raymond Hitchcock	XIII Ben Bernie
IV Will Hayes	VII Tom Wise	X Eddie Cantor	XIV Joe Laurie, Jr.

with stars. George M. Cohan was still the abbot, George Jessel was the dean, Harry Hershfield the secretary, and just a few of the important names who were then proud to be members were the Honorable Al Smith, Honorable James J. Walker, Joe Cook, Rudy Vallee, Bing Crosby, Harry Richman, George Jessel, Irving Berlin, Sam Harris, Max Gordon, Paul Whiteman, Gus Van, Dr. Hugo Riesenfeld, Robert L. Ripley, Charlie Foy, Eddie Foy, William Morris, Sr., Lionel Atwill, Harry Rose, Ben Piermont, Eddie Dowling, George Burns, Lou Holtz, Will Rogers, Bobby Clark, Lester Allen, Bert Lahr, Jack Benny, S. Jay Kaufman, Maurice Chevalier, and Jesse Lasky.

Despite this galaxy they couldn't save the club. The Depression attacked show business first. Many of the stars listened to Greeley and went West looking for greener dollars and bigger parts. Some left show business to try their talents at other things. Other members couldn't pay their dues. Still others who were left couldn't get up enough scratch to pay the mortgage and the bills. The Friars were bankrupt.

Producers Sam Harris and Max Gordon scrambled to put together the Friars Frolic of 1932. It starred Harry Hershfield, Pat Rooney, Georgie Price, Jans and Whalen, the three Samuels brothers, Eddie Leonard, Walter C. Kelly, and Joe Frisco. It was MC'd by George M. Cohan himself. It headlined guest of honor James J. Walker himself. Still they couldn't make enough to pay the rent.

The Friars were out of business. A handful of the faithful stuck with it. They moved to a small loft over Lindy's restaurant and there the waters were even more troubled. In 1935 their then executive secretary, an in-hock horseplayer named Charles Pope, absconded with whatever they had left. He couldn't face the bookies or the Friars so he skipped, leaving the club holding the empty bag. After Lindy's it was a suite at the Astor Hotel and then the owner of the Edison Hotel, Max Kramer, who was a show-business buff, gave them a room at the Edison Hall on West 47th Street. These weren't exactly clubrooms—they were really card-rooms with a little show business thrown in between hands—and the members kept moving about like out-of-work actors making the rounds.

Meanwhile they had the classiest temporary meeting hall in captivity. The Central Park West apartment of Ted Lewis with its vaulted ceilings, stained-glass windows, and parquet floors, plus its wall-to-wall inventory of food and its three live-in help, was a welcome bunk.

Besides the eight-room apartment that they moved into in 1931, the Lewises had a house in Elberon, New Jersey, which boasted fifteen bedrooms, give or take a few plus dormitories—one for the gents, one for the ladies—plus a private dining room just for the staff of thirteen. Thus, to the Lewises feeding an army of Friars was not exactly a hardship.

Ted, who was the herald of the Friars (an appointed, not an elected, job), was a devotee of the club. Every Monday and Wednesday he took dinner there and played cards until the early hours. When there was no club—only cardrooms—he moved the "boys" up to his place. The "boys" included Damon Runyon, Mike Todd, songwriter Benny Davis, stockbroker Stanley Garfinkel, singer Benny Fields, Jack Benny, Eddie Cantor who loved to kibitz, etc. On these stag nights the bedrooms, library, dining room, and large living room dominated by Ted's portrait would house over a dozen bridge tables with round tops and maybe fifty guys would sit down to a friendly game.

The buffet was no greasy brown paper-bag job from the local deli either. There was a butler on duty all through the night plus the caterers and extra waiters and bartenders so the "boys" could stuff themselves on lobster Newburg and roast beef on those little informal stag nights that the Friars lumbered up to Club Lewis. Lewis, a born gambler, loved poker, gin, pinochle, the dice at Vegas, anything. The card games would grind on sometimes until ten in the morning.

When the Friars moved into permanent clubrooms, Friar Ted Lewis once again became a permanent fixture. In fact, his last night out was spent at the Friars. Monday night, August 23, 1971, Ted was, as usual, at the club. He wasn't hungry and complained that for some reason the liver didn't taste as good as always. Tuesday he felt poorly and the doctor came over. Ted and his Adah spent a quiet night at home watching TV in the library. At nine the next morning Friar Ted Lewis was gone.

A few weeks later his widow received a check for over $200 from Walter Goldstein—Ted's winnings from the last night of his life.

When the floating clubroom finally found an anchor, Operation Ted Lewis became a page in Friar history.

Coincidentally, with Milton Berle becoming abbot in 1945, the Friars started to make a comeback. The nightclubs and theatres were on the way up again, TV had brought a lot of stars back to New York, and Uncle Miltie, King of Television, led the Friars back to the limelight. In 1949 the roast to Milton at the Latin Quarter gave the brothers a little spending money. In 1950 a roast for Joe E. Lewis at the Waldorf-Astoria partially defrayed the indebtedness on the new Monastery at 123 West 56th. In 1951 Jesse Block of Block and Sully inveigled his pal Jack Benny into being the fall guy. Jack was very hot on radio and Friar Block knew Benny would attract the show-business crowd, the newspaper guys, and the moneyed hangers-on back to the fold. George Jessel was booked to preside. Jessel was the official roastmaster. Earl Wilson dubbed him the toastmaster general of the United States and he was so appointed by six presidents. As Georgie admitted at the Benny dinner, "I have functioned at every known affair that was given this year. I have run the gamut. I have spoken at a eulogy in Pittsburgh, the launching of a destroyer at the harbor of San Pedro, and at a circumcision in Glendale—all in one day—and fortunately I was able to use the same speech at all three occasions. I will now use the same address in introducing our guest of honor, Jack Benny."

The mayor of Waukegan, Illinois, Jack's hometown, was invited to make the address. When the mayor copped out, Jesse substituted the governor of Illinois. Nobody knew who the hell the governor was when he showed up but he stole the show and the headlines. His name was Adlai Stevenson and he was slotted on the bill following Fred Allen. Fred was never funnier—especially for a show-business audience. Also, they were cheering him because he had just lost his TV show. Allen started on NBC first: "If the U.S.A. can get along with one VP—I don't understand why NBC needs twenty-six." Now he turned to Jack Benny: "He's the only Friar who would

A Friars Frolic rehearsal with Paul Webster, George Gershwin, Seymour Felix, and Lou Alter at the piano.

travel 3,000 miles for a free meal—I don't want to say he's cheap, but he's got short arms and carries his money low in his pockets—there is a saying, 'You can't take it with you,' but if you see a funeral procession with a Brink's armored car behind the hearse, you'll know Jack is having a try at it. Now if the guest of honor is seen sitting up, then we'll know it's not a funeral." Allen recalled their struggling days in vaudeville: "One date in Centralia, Illinois, that is, a *suburb* of Centralia, Illinois, stands out in my memory. It was a wonderful little town! I remember the mayor was an elk—a real elk. Jack was next to closing on a two-act bill. The theatre was so far back in the woods that the manager was a bear. He paid the acts off in honey." Fred ended with a compliment: "I love Jack Benny—I have no taste, but I love him."

Fred finished to a thunderous ovation. Jessel next introduced Adlai Stevenson. Most of the audience and the committee didn't know if Adlai was a boy or a girl—they didn't know whether to present him with cigars or a corsage. George said as he presented him, "After Fred Allen, I wouldn't give this spot to a leopard."

The unknown governor weakly rose to his feet and said, "Gentlemen, before this meeting I was out in the men's room talking to Mr. Allen and he confessed to me that he didn't have a speech for tonight's occasion. Now, his business is comedy and I'm only in politics so I felt sorry for him. I graciously gave him my speech. So you have just heard it. Good night, everybody." And he sat down.

The Jack Benny dinner was the turning point. After that it was Bob Hope who was honored, then Jessel himself, and the Friars were on top again.

November 1957 the brothers moved into their present friary at 57 East 55th Street. A decision that just barely squeaked through the board of governors was made to allow women—not as members, but as guests of members—and then only at night and for Saturday lunch. So the boys (if you'll pardon the expression) still have five days a week to make like monks.

In the good old days before vaudeville became just a word in the dictionary the Friars Club was a necessary part of an actor's life. It didn't merely pander to his pleasure. It served his need. It was the local candy store, the corner pub, the factory lunchroom, the church social hall. It was the place to go when there was no place to go.

Show people don't all live on the same street. There's no such

The Friars X-rated luncheon for Lou Holtz. Seated left to right, *Lou Nelson, Joe E. Lewis, Sammy Davis, Jr., Lou Holtz, Walter Winchell, Lew Parker, Dean Harry Delf, and assorted comics and politicians including Alan King, Jack E. Leonard, Phil Foster, and Bobby Gordon.*

thing as a glitter ghetto. They migrate to the metropolitan area from Connecticut, New Jersey, New York, Long Island, and their in-laws' place in the Bronx, or from train stations, bus depots, and airports. The guys in greasepaint are itinerants. And the Friars Club is *their* local candy store, corner pub, factory lunchroom, and neighborhood social hall all rolled up in one.

In them good old days it was even more needful because it was their *only* place to go. That was when an actor was an actor. He wasn't an actor and a businessman. He was just a plain actor—sometimes great, sometimes lousy—but an actor. Just an actor. Today the actor is twelve other things. The leading man also owns the picture and the star comedian also produces the telecast and the Italian singer also is the packager who books the rest of the show. It's a different show business.

In those glory days an actor's office was the nearest telephone.

At the Friars Monastery. From left to right, *Phil Reagan, Eddie Cantor, Milton Berle, and Benny Fields rehearsing for a nervous breakdown.*

He didn't do the business. He didn't go to an office with a telex and a Xerox from nine to five to oversee his business because he had business guys who did the business. On a day-to-day basis when he was between bookings he had no place to go.

When he wasn't onstage being a star he was at home being a nothing. What good is it to know you're a star when around the house you're a bum? What good is it to have your name up in lights when the maid is shoving you out so she can vacuum? The only answer is to gather up your dignity and your clippings and go off to your club. The Friars was a necessity.

Today's actors are office types. This isn't the guy who hangs around the house and sees his wife every day. It's the guy who never hangs around the house and never sees his wife any day— except at the Friars at Saturday lunch.

As the decades dissolved one into another, even the complexion of the regulars changed. The biggies moved into the movies and pushed West: Groucho, Jessel, Cantor, Burns, Benny, Durante, Harry Richman, Hope, Martin and Lewis. Some wound up around the round table at the L.A. Friars, others at Hillcrest. When the Ed Sullivan show took its final bow and assorted TV variety shows moved Westward Ho! and the Strand, Paramount, Roxy, Loew's State, and Capitol theatres went dark, the next wave climbed into their covered wagons with the whitewall tires and it was good-bye to Jack Carter, Buddy Hackett, Marty Allen, Joey Bishop, Red Buttons, Steve Allen.

The Copa went, the Latin Quarter went, and Pat Cooper, Jerry Vale, Harry James, Sergio Franchi, Phil Silvers, Peter Lind Hayes, and Totie Fields also went. To Vegas. They can be found around the roulette tables. When the Borscht Belt shrunk to the Concord Hotel on July Fourth weekend or Grossinger's on New Year's Eve, it was curtains for Jerry Lester, Mickey Rooney, stand-up comics like Eddie Schaefer, Leon Fields, Buddy Walker, and those who transplanted in Miami and formed the Footlighters Club and can be found around a beach.

From the fifties to the seventies it was the modern-day Diaspora. They left Broadway, Times Square, 42nd Street—the homeland— and made it to heathen ground. The young ones emigrated to L.A. to try for a series on TV or the big screen; the names fled to Vegas to be near their money; the second bananas picked Florida for the easy life; the giants settled into mansions and gardners in Beverly Hills.

And yet the Friars in this contemporary era has flourished.

When 55th Street opened it numbered about 200 members. Today it's over a thousand. It's still the place for performers who are single or to grab a little shoptalk and exchange lies with other performers. It's still the place to catch your agent who is hiding from you when he's in his inside office but can't hide anything from you when he's in the steam room at the club. It's still the place for up-and-comers who find it a warm retreat from their cold hotel rooms, and the big names who need a room full of fellow actors and fans and the used-to-bes who need a platform to tell those rusty stories of when they were about-to-bes.

And added to the large membership of business managers, financial managers, personal managers, club-date agents, TV commercial agents, public-relations guys, and the fellas who put the caps on the teeth of the fellas who smile on TV, we still have the top bananas who drop by when they're in town. Many a lunch day you'll spot a Tom Jones, George Burns, George Raft, Alan King, and believe it or not even Henny Youngman—the king of the one-liners—if you don't include Moses.

3

The Chairs

I was sitting in the dining room the other Saturday lunchtime with my friend Walter Goldstein, the executive director, and his assistant, Jean-Pierre Trebot. Naturally, we were talking about the old times. "They're better now," Walter was telling his young assistant, "it's a blend of the old and the new. There's George Burns trading anecdotes with a new young comic, Freddie Roman, and Engelbert Humperdinck at the Round Table with the Tom Jones of the 'Stone Age,' Rudy Vallee." He gazed around the room, "And there's Henny Youngman sitting with his old gag writer and new agent." "And Gene Baylos," I added, "is sitting with his back toward the check."

Jean-Pierre was reading the chairs in the main room, each of which bears a plaque in memory of a former member who is now doing his act for Saint Peter. "Say," mused Jean-Pierre, "I never met Ben Bernie, Eddie Cantor, Fred Allen, Al Jolson, W. C. Fields, John Philip Sousa, Will Rogers, or those other glorious names on the chairs. I'd love to have been here when they were around—if only those chairs could talk."

"Y'know something?" reflected Walter, "their stories will last forever. They'll be around a hell of a lot longer than those chairs will."

"How about that one—Al Kelly—who was he?" Jean-Pierre asked. "He was the king of double-talk," I explained, "and he worked in my act for years." Then I had to figure out a way of explaining what double-talk is. "It's like reading an eye chart. It's fractured English is what it is. If you should meet someone who introduces himself with something that sounds like 'I am Charley Imglick and I'd like to Javlin with my liebst. Can you get me a rabinat or a flang?' don't blame the acoustics. You have just been introduced to double-talk."

Except for a handful of pros like Cliff Nazarro, Sid Gary, and Al Kelly, most of the art was used for play or rib rather than profes-

24

sionally. Gary loved to put everybody on. Once he tried to snow a new waiter. "I'll have two filbers and a cup of coffee," he said. A few minutes later the waiter was back and gave him this: "Sorry, we're out of filbers—how about crullers?"

"We lost a good waiter once because of this double-talk," Walter told us. "Al Kelly was sitting at the table having lunch with Ted Lewis, Goodman Ace, Myron Cohen, and a group of other Friars of various shapes, billing, and gags when the waiter approached with pad and pencil in hand.

His luck he had to hit Al Kelly first. "I'll have a fried blatz on the raybone," Al said, "and make sure it's well done—and don't put any ralts on it—and I'll have some hooytey on the side, please." The waiter stood there poised. He figured he had a table full of other orders and what the hell he'd come back to this foreigner later. "What'll you have?" he asked Myron Cohen who was sitting next to Al. "I'll have the same as my friend," he said, pointing to Kelly.

"We haven't seen the waiter since," grinned Walter.

The Jack E. Leonard chair brought a thousand of his snarls to my memory. Anybody that sat down at the Round Table was a target. Sinatra screamed when Jack E. praised, "You got a great voice there, kid; too bad it hasn't reached your throat." To Steve Allen he snarled, "Some day you'll go too far and I hope you'll stay there." To Don Rickles: "You got a nice personality but not for a human being." One afternoon Jack E. was stopped and by, of all people, the lovable comedy actor Hugh Herbert. Herbert was smoking a cigar and Jack E. growled, "Don't you ever inhale?" and Herbert zinged, "Not with *you* in the room."

Jack E.'s mouth could easily have been declared a lethal weapon and, when he was in the mood to barb, you couldn't soften him even with flattery. I once heard Ed Sullivan say to him, "You look pretty good—that's a nice sunburn. How did you get it?" And Jack E. bellowed, "I got a lousy agent."

"Didn't any of them ever get insulted at Jack?" Jean-Pierre asked.

"No," Walter answered, "they loved it. Fat Jack, which is what we all used to call him, went from table to table sticking the needle into everybody and they ate it up. One time Julius La Rosa took me aside and asked, 'Tell me, is Fat Jack angry at me?' I asked why and Julius explained, 'Because I passed him three times and he was very pleasant—he didn't louse me up once!' "

Harry Hershfield's chair could tell some beautiful stories. He

New York City hails the Friars while Alan King and Jack E. Leonard attempt to steal the sign.

was a friend of the immediate world. He knew everybody from the busboys at the club to the president of the United States. Somehow everything always happened to Harry on his way to the Friars or Lambs. About ten years ago a broad stopped him just as he was about to enter the Friary or maybe it was the Lambery. Anyhow, as Harry told it she asked him, "Would you like to have a good time?" Harry told her there were three reasons why he couldn't. "First, I have no money. . . ." She yelled back, "You can stick the other two."

Harry escorted the great Bernard Baruch to the Round Table one Monday. On their way over they met a couple of out-of-work actors who needed a little friendship. Harry invited them for lunch in spite of the fact that they weren't wearing ties and looked pretty shabby. When the maître d' protested their appearance, Mr. Baruch ran interference. "It's my fault—I can't help it—I bought a new hearing aid and the union makes me carry two electricians with me wherever I go."

A waiter carrying a tray with two chef salads and an omelet

moved a few feet to his right and my eye fell on the Fred Allen chair. "I was sitting at the Round Table a few hundred years ago," I told them, "when John Francis Sullivan, better known as Fred Allen, strolled in. He was working at Loew's State and it seems he had run into a really tough Monday matinee audience. 'How did it go,' I asked, as he sat down. 'Did you kill them?' 'No,' growled Fred, 'they were dead when I got there.'"

"Isn't it odd," Jean-Pierre remarked, "that Mr. Jack Benny's chair and Mr. Fred Allen's chair are side by side? I remember when I was a little boy and heard them on the radio, they were always feuding—did they really hate each other?"

"No," Jesse Block said as he joined us at the table, "they had great respect for each other and were close friends. That feud started accidentally. Fred had some six-year-old kid on his show playing the violin. The kid hit a dozen clinkers and Fred ad-libbed when he was through, 'This kid gives lessons to Jack Benny.' Then he added, 'By the way, have you heard Jack recently? He raises millions for the musicians' union—just by threatening to play. Now when he opens his violin case—the audience hopes there's a machine gun in it.' That was the start of something new. Back in California Jack heard about it and asked his writer Harry Conn to ad-lib an answer for him. That was Wednesday night. On Sunday night Benny came up with, 'You can't see Fred Allen's face until you lift the bags under his eyes. And with that pained expression, he looks like a hen trying to lay a square egg.'

"Then, of course, Nat Hiken, Fred's writer, put a few barbs in Allen's next script: 'Jack Benny is the only fiddler who makes you feel that the strings would sound better back in the cat.' On Benny's show he countered with: 'Fred Allen looks good in front of everything but a mirror. He's the star of stage, screen, and radio—so whether you go out or not he's got you trapped!'

"When Fred Allen came to bat Wednesday, he opened his program with, 'The first time I saw Jack Benny he was doing a monologue onstage at a vaudeville theatre in Ohio. He had a pig onstage with him—the pig was there to eat up the stuff the audience threw at him.'

"When they met here at the Friars, and like I told you they loved each other, they continued the feud just for laughs. One lunchtime when they were both in town Jack said to Fred as he joined the table, 'Are we going to have a battle of wits today?' And Fred answered, "It's against my principles to fight an unarmed man—anyway, you couldn't ad-lib a belch after a Hungarian dinner.' And Jack said, 'You wouldn't talk that way to me if I had my writers with me.'"

What Jean-Pierre didn't know was that Jack Benny had been a way of life for Jesse Block. They were a love affair. They were part of an eight-way love affair going back almost to when there were gas lamps instead of footlights in a theatre: Eddie Cantor and Ida, Jack and Mary Livingstone Benny, Jesse Block and his partner Eve Sully, and Gracie Allen and her partner Nat (or George as he was called professionally) Burns.

Back to the early days of vaudeville, to the drafty dressing rooms, lousy food, tank towns, sleeping in trains—back to the lean years went this friendship of eight: Eddie and Ida, Jack and Mary, Jesse and Eve, George and Gracie. Eddie and Ida are long gone. Gracie is gone. And now Jack. Only half of them were left. When Jack went it was too much for Jesse Block. He wrote a tearful letter to his friend George Burns and a year later he showed me George's answer. It was dated January 30, 1975. It said in part:

Dear Jesse—

I got your very sad letter, and I'll tell you a little secret that might help you. It helped me a lot. When Gracie died I used to go to Forest Lawn and see her every week. I'd sit in the mausoleum and look up at where she is, and I'd cry. Well, you can only cry so many weeks, then you stop crying. And every time I went to see her I used to tell her everything. Gracie has been gone eleven years, and I still go there. But now I tell her little humorous things that have happened to me. Who knows. Maybe she can hear me, and she always thought I was funny.

Anyway, Jesse, what I'm trying to tell you is you just can't stay sad. Life must go on, and there's nothing you can do about it. I know how close you and Jack were, but look, you still got Eve, you still got yourself. There's nothing you can do about it, it's the only game in town. I even spoke to Jack's manager, Irving Fein, he's a very smart fellow, and he told me there's no other exit—that's it.

A few lines about what he was doing professionally and then Burns signed it "Nat."

There were a lot of things that this kid, Jean-Pierre, didn't know. And who was going to tell him? I was thinking about all the things that he didn't know when a doctor with a show-business clientele

Left, *Jack E. Leonard, Ed Sullivan, and Don Rickles at the Sullivan roast.* Right, *Joe E. Lewis, Jimmy Durante, and Walter Winchell rehearsing for a Friars roast.*

hoisted himself out of the Eddie Cantor chair and it brought another rash of reminiscences from Jesse Block. "That Izzie Itskowitz was the nicest," he said. "He got in trouble for going after Father Coughlin who was attacking the Jews, y'know. He lost his radio show because the agency said the sponsors didn't want a controversial personality connected with their products. He was blacklisted until Jack Benny called the agency and insisted they put Cantor back on the air."

"Irving Mansfield told me a beautiful story about Cantor and his pal Georgie Jessel," I interjected. "They were on the same bill on a vaudeville unit. When they arrived in town, Jessel saw the billing which read: 'Eddie Cantor with Georgie Jessel.' Georgie berated manager Mansfield, 'What kind of conjunction is that—Eddie Cantor *with* Georgie Jessel?' Irving promised to fix it. The next day the marquee read: 'Eddie Cantor *but* Georgie Jessel.'"

Jesse reminded us that Jessel was always broke and Cantor had millions. Georgie enjoyed blaming it on booze and broads but still it bugged him that Cantor was such a good businessman. There was that afternoon he walked out of his dressing-room door and saw a huge sign with the legend "Jesus Saves." Under it he wrote in ink: "But not like Cantor."

There are endless stories about actors—that species of humanity that will wear a toupee but not glasses and a dress suit with a torn shirt.

"To me this is the best actors' story in the world," Walter said:

29

"There's a chair here someplace with the name Bert Frohman on it. I used to love him in vaudeville. One time he opened in Baltimore to an empty house. There were only *six* people in the audience. It was disaster. When Bert returned to the Round Table he admitted to the guys, 'It was a horrible experience—only *seven* people in the audience.'"

Coming back from a phone call I noticed I was sitting in the Will Rogers chair. "Everybody in the Friars treasured him," I began, "because he understood us. 'A comedian's job is the toughest,' Will used to say, 'his option comes up after every joke.' Rogers had a humor that withstands the sands of time. He told a group at the table one night, 'Congressmen are the real comedians—every time they make a law, it's a joke—and every time they make a joke, it's a law.'"

"I'm glad to say I at least knew Ed Sullivan," Jean-Pierre said, stroking the back of Jesse Block's chair. "He was really a good guy," put in Jesse. "Ed always came in looking for actors to recruit for his charities. I remember knocking off three benefits with him in one day. Eve and I, Sammy Davis, Jr., Robert Merrill, and Jack Benny —we all played a Catholic breakfast at the Commodore, a Protestant fund-raising luncheon at the Waldorf, and a synagogue at night. 'You should be proud this day,' Eddie said to us after the last show, 'you just played God across the board!'"

"For somebody from Port Chester, New York, he did pretty good," Walter said, "and he produced a lot of his shows from his table right here in the dining room. There are dozens of former stars who couldn't get a job until he gave them a shot and started them back up again—like Smith and Dale, Benny Fields, Blossom Seeley, and so many others."

"He was a good sportswriter and columnist for the *Evening Mail,* then *Graphic,* and finally the New York *Daily News,*" I reminded them, "before he went on TV. But he'll be remembered best by the good he did for people. I have to tell you about the benefit I did with Bob Hope when Ed insisted we join him at Saint Albans Hospital to bring a little cheer to the veterans coming home from Vietnam. 'One thing they don't want is sympathy,' Bob explained. 'When I walk into a ward filled with kids who can't get out of bed and are harnessed to contraptions, I usually say, 'That's okay, fellows, you don't have to get up for me.'

"When we got to Saint Albans, Bob warned the eight show girls we brought along, 'No sympathy. Don't tell them how great they are and what they did for the country—the sacrifices they made— just throw the funny lines.' Coming down the corridor toward the first ward we heard singing—but like at the top of someone's voice. As we entered we saw the 'crooner' pushing himself toward us in a wheelchair—by the power of his arms—the only limbs he had left. He laughed and hollered, 'Hello, Bob Hope—hello, Ed Sullivan— look at all the beautiful girls.'

" 'Just a minute,' Bob greeted him, 'what's with the singing and laughs? We're here to entertain you! What the hell are you doing meeting us with a song?'

"His answer did more for us than we could ever do for him: 'When I stopped looking at what I had lost and began looking at all the goodies I got left—I can see—I can hear—I can even grab one of those beautiful girls you brought—I can put out my hands and thank you for coming—I realize I have a lot to be grateful for.'

"When we got back to the club, Ed thanked us, 'If you do a good job for others, you heal yourself at the same time because a dose of joy is a spiritual cure. It transcends all barriers.' "

"I loved Bob's story—the one that happened at an officers' club. After a pointless and blasphemous story, an alleged comic noticed all eyes were suddenly fastened on the collar insignia of a pleasant, quiet clergyman at the end of the table. 'Fr' crissake,' blustered the storyteller, 'are you a chaplain?' With a light smile and deliberate emphasis, the chaplain answered, 'Yes, for Christ's sake, I am.' "

Amidst the noisy good-byes of the table to my right I suddenly noticed that the George M. Cohan chair was empty. Seemed symbolic. For a long while that's how it had been.

It started August 1919 when Equity, the actors' union, called its first strike. In this case we can't say that the actors were struck by lightning because lightning was struck by the actors. The first production the young union marched against was a show called *Lightning*. In 1900 when Equity's forerunner, an infant union named The White Rats (which derived its name from star spelled backwards), took its first step, George M. moved against it. With his friend Edward F. Albee, emperor of the vaudeville houses, he joined forces with management.

"I will never do business with this Actors Equity Association," he is quoted as saying at the time. "Every dollar I have in the world—

and I have a few—is on the table in this fight against actors that are being misled by Equity. I would be with the actors if they were right but I know they're wrong."

Cohan pledged $100,000 of his own money to form his own Actors' Fidelity League (alias FIDO) and recruited stars—Ina Claire, Janet Beecher, David Warfield, William Collier, Louis Mann, E. H. Sothern—to battle the union. Actor-producer-owner George M. found that the bread-and-butter actors hated the producer-owner in him. The fight was bitter. Even his fellow Friars took sides against him. The wounds went deep. Cohan resigned from his beloved Friars as well as the Lambs and vowed never to set foot in either again. Many of the faithful marched on the George M. Cohan-Sam Harris Theatre on 42nd Street to urge him to change his mind but the playwright in him had determined to write the ending.

His friend E. F. Albee wrote about Cohan in this Friar-to-Friar message: "There is one blot on this splendid club. It did not stand by this good man at a time when he needed its support. I say to the members that when a man like George M. Cohan represents

Toastmaster George Jessel, Abbot Milton Berle, Guest of Honor Bob Hope, with Elder Statesman Bernard Baruch, and Veep Alben W. Barkley.

you, works for your interest, is interested in your welfare, stand by him, whether he is right or wrong. He has served you. He has been and is now your friend.

"The Friars is a great institution. We need clubs, particularly in show business where good fellowship abounds and where charity is disbursed . . . The theatrical members of the Friars represent a wonderful business. . . . We should all strive to elevate our profession, to keep high its standard, improve its ethics, extend its charities, look after its unfortunate. Stand by each other. Let the future wipe out our past misdeeds, make us unselfish in our thoughts and actions, and keep in remembrance that the Friars Club represents an ancient order which was founded in the love and service of God."

The George M. Cohan who once cracked, "If you're living outside of New York, you're living in a tent—anywhere outside of New York is Bridgeport," spent very little time in New York after that. He couldn't face the friends who hadn't stuck with him. He spent most of his time in the country writing plays and puttering in the garden. An actor asked him then how he liked the country and Cohan replied, "If I had to live in New York City I am sure my life would be wider—but not so long."

It took a very long time for the wound to heal. George M. never joined Equity and is still a blot on that union but he did return to his Friars and was reelected as abbot. He served faithfully and lovingly for a lengthy second term.

In 1958 the proposal that a statue be erected to George M. Cohan in Manhattan's Duffy Square was sent to Ralph Bellamy, as the head of the Actors Equity Association, by producer Max Gordon. Gordon suggested that "while George Cohan and Equity had their differences, the fact still remains that George made a great contribution to the theatre and gave work to hundreds of actors in plays that he wrote and produced. During his lifetime he was most generous in his contributions to the needy in the theatrical profession." Max ended with a request for a generous contribution from AEA for the project.

Angus Duncan, Equity's executive secretary, replied by agreeing that George "was a dominant figure in our theatre and contributed immeasurably to it and its traditions—as an author, director, songwriter, producer, as well as actor . . . and so the council concluded that indeed the bitterness of the past should be forgotten . . ."

Enclosed was a check to the George M. Cohan Memorial Committee in the amount equal to a life membership in the union, $240.

Back came a letter from Oscar Hammerstein 2nd. In referring to the check, his letter says that it "carries with it an ironical suggestion that a few stray grains of bitterness remain. I remember the old situation very well indeed, and I do not dispute your right to continue a resentment so deep. I must, however, refuse to cooperate with you in pinpricking George's ghost. I am therefore returning the check, thanking you for your sincere but unsuccessful effort to forget."

On Friday evening, September 11, 1959, when the George M. Cohan memorial statue was unveiled in Duffy Square it was done with the help and fund raising of the Friars in memory of their former abbot.

Robert Moses, talking for the City of New York, said at the unveiling:

"It is no mere accident that George M. Cohan is placed here so close to our beloved Father Duffy. Here they stand on a little island in the midst of swirling traffic by day, floodlights at night, and eerie silence in the early morning, both typical city men, both unhyphenated Americans, the one with the song on his lips, the other with the lantern in his hand, one the minstrel with the jaunty cane, the other the priest in uniform standing squarely before the Celtic Cross. Here, you scoffers at Gotham and Broadway, are the symbols of the true New York."

4

F-F-Friar
J-J-Joe F-F-Frisco

A bunch of the boys were whooping it up at the Friars saloon. And they were the biggest guns in town. It was a pretty classy group even for the Round Table. There was Aaron Chwatt, Irwin Kniberg, Julius Marx, Nathan Birnbaum, Benny Kubelsky, William Breitbard, and Joseph Abramowitz.

Maybe these names don't sound like they could jazz up a marquee or draw a buck and a quarter at the box office, but Aaron Chwatt boasts an Oscar bigger than himself under the name of Red Buttons. Irwin Kniberg as Alan King gets over a hundred thousand a week in Vegas. Julius Marx and his brothers Chico, Harpo, and Zeppo didn't do too bad in pictures. Nathan Birnbaum got himself a wife and a partner by the name of Gracie Allen. Benny Kubelsky and his wife Sadye were the hottest thing on radio under the names of Jack Benny and Mary Livingstone. William Breitbard is the WNEW radio star and TV personality William B. Williams. Joseph Abramowitz is the modest and humble goodwill ambassador, comedian, and author who is writing this story.

The subject at this particular session was the stuttering comic Joe Frisco.

First I think I should tell you what is a Joe Frisco. He was a headliner in vaudeville in the days when Fanny was a girl's name. In that era no program was complete without a monologist like Frank Tinney, William Collier, Will Rogers, Walter C. Kelly, Bert Williams, and great song and dance men like Eddie Leonard and comedy teams like Weber and Fields, Duffy and Sweeney, Van and Schenck, and Healy and Cross. Frisco was the headliner comedian.

Joe Frisco was in the era of *Guys and Dolls*. He knew from nothing about the outside world. His world was bounded on the east by the bookies and on the west by the ponies. He was a Damon Runyon original. With all the money he made, he never had a penny.

It all went to the horses. And Frisco made money. He was always working. In those days you could stay on the road for two or three years straight with the same act. Any savvy performer could get fifty weeks or more of vaudeville just in and around New York. Then, if you stuck in a new joke or two and maybe changed your suit or derby, the agents would send you out for another couple of years. Joe Frisco never changed his act or his derby. His only expense was the cigar he used in his act, but he still worked all the time—how else could he stay in good with the touts and book-makers?

The big time was the Keith, Orpheum, Pantages, Loew's, and Interstate Time. These could keep you working for five years. That's besides the split weeks in the little circuits like the Dow time, the Butterfield time, and the Sablosky and McGurk route. Joe worked them all.

The Palace Theatre on Broadway was more important to a performer than the palaces in England, Thailand, and Persia combined, and Joe Frisco was a steady tenant there too. The trouble was everything went to the nags. He only worked in show business to get the money to put into his real business—the horses.

With the end of Prohibition and the dying gasp of the two-a-day plus the beginning of the five and six shows a day at the giant theatres along Broadway's Rialto, Joe Frisco segued into nightclubs. After all, he couldn't spend all that time away from the track! Joe settled down in Hollywood near a horse room and a friend who spotlighted him in her club, Grace Hayes's Lodge in the Valley.

Some philosopher once said—it was either Aristotle or Plato or maybe it was Nick the Greek: "Gambling is a sure way of getting nothing for something." Well, Frisco, unlike his other vaudeville pals, Bing Crosby, Jimmy Durante of Clayton, Jackson, and Durante, the Ritz Brothers, Eddie Foy, Eddie Cantor, and George M. Cohan, finished up completely broke. At the end he had nothing but a great wit and a sense of humor.

"I loved him," Jack Benny addressed the Round Table. "He was one of a kind. My favorite Frisco story is the one where Joe had hit upon lean times. It became his custom to stand in front of the Brown Derby hoping to find an old acquaintance who might buy him a meal. Almost everybody loved Joe and when they saw him outside the Derby they would all say, 'Hey, Joe, how about a cup of coffee?' After a dozen such invites Joe remarked, 'D-D-Don't anybody ever eat m-m-meat in there?'"

FRIARS LEAVE ON FIRST TRANSCONTINENTAL TOUR! Chief of Police Mulrooney of New York, in the absence of Mayor James J. Walker, bids the traveling Friars bon voyage as they leave on their first transcontinental jaunt. In the group you'll recognize: Pat Rooney and Pat 3rd; Harry Hershfield; Joe Frisco (with cigar); Jans and Whalen; Danny Dare; Walter C. Kelly; Joseph E. Howard; Buddy Doyle; Eddie Leonard and Eddie Jr.

George Burns reminded us of the time he took the stuttering comic on a tour of Hollywood and showed him the scenery. " 'Look at those beautiful hills,' I squealed, 'look at that beautiful Pacific Ocean!' 'Y-Y-Yeah,' Joe said, 'b-b-but you can't put k-k-ketchup on 'em.' "

Red Buttons told about the time Frisco bought a painting of *The Last Supper* at an actor's charity function. Later, after a few bad days at the track, he took the painting to a pawnshop. The broker looked at it and said he didn't know too much about *Last Supper* paintings. "What do you think it's worth?" "Well," said Joe, "at least t-t-ten dollars a p-p-plate."

Groucho said, "I once tried to get Joe to put his money in a safer gamble. I took him to a stockbroker's office on the top floor of a Wall Street skyscraper. The broker was showing off. He proudly pointed to the panorama of New York Bay and asked Joe to notice the dozen or more yachts that belonged to big-shot brokers. 'Great' Joe said, 'b-b-but where are the c-c-customers' yachts?' "

William B. told us of the time Mickey Rooney suggested to Frisco: "You seem so unhappy, why don't you see my analyst?" "L-L-Listen, Mickey," said Joe, "I refuse to p-p-pay anyone fifty dollars an hour j-j-just to squeal on my mother."

Alan King remembered one of the classic Frisco tales: "Broadway has a thousand stories about actors fighting hysterically for proper billing and prestigious salaries. Joe was once flatter than usual but still unyielding in his insistence that he get $3,500 a week at the Palace. 'I can get you $2,500 a week,' an agent coaxed. 'You know my p-p-price . . . thirty f-f-five hundred,' retorted Joe from his room at the Edison Hotel where he was carrying on his battle of independence. 'I might get you $3,000,' said the agent. 'I s-s-said th-th-thirty five,' answered Joe. 'Come down to Lindy's and let's talk about it,' the agent begged. 'Wh-Wh-What? And get l-l-locked out of my room?' said Joe."

I submitted my favorite. It happened on November 26, 1916. It was the Friars Frolic in honor of Enrico Caruso in the Great Hall of the Monastery. The Friars' abbot, George M. Cohan, was the toastmaster, Friars Victor Herbert and Charles Emerson Cook wrote a special song for the occasion that has become the anthem of the club, and Irving Berlin arranged the entertainment, which included Al Jolson, John Barrymore, and Enrico Caruso himself.

Into this setting ambled the young vaudevillian Joe Frisco. Every hotshot in town was waiting patiently backstage to get on. Big as they were they each had a respect for Caruso that amounted to awe. The famous opera star stood in the wings waiting his turn, but nobody actually had the courage to address the great man himself —that is, nobody but Frisco. "Hey, C-C-Caruso," he nudged, "d-d-don't do 'D-D-Darktown Strutters' Ball'—that's my number and I follow you."

By the time we had finished telling these gems, the Round Table was pressed down and running over with Frisco stories from every Friar in town. The number one Friscophile is a beautiful guy called Peter Lind Hayes who just happened to be visiting in New York from his home in Las Vegas.

"Joe was working at my mother's club, Grace Hayes's Lodge in Hollywood," Peter told us, "and as usual was across the street in the diner laying bets. It was a celebrity night and Mom introduced Lawrence Tibbett. The world-renowned baritone started to sing his famous 'Glory Road' and his magnificent voice was booming around the room as Joe entered. 'Now, th-th-there's a guy with a v-v-voice,' he marveled as he approached my mother, 'wh-wh-why don't you sign him up and p-p-put him in the show?' 'You dope,' Mom explained, 'that man's name is Lawrence Tibbett.' 'Th-Th-The hell with it!' screamed Frisco, 'ch-change his n-n-name—put him in the show!'"

Goodman Ace showed up with the story of the tout who was complaining to Joe that he hadn't won a single race either with or for a wealthy sucker. "He gives me a thousand dollars a race to bet for him," he cried, "and I've given him twenty-three straight losers." "G-G-Get away from that b-b-bum," snarled Frisco, "h-he's unlucky for you."

Milton Berle was on the fifth floor in the sauna room taking a steam bath when he heard the laughs all the way downstairs on the main floor. He turned the steam up as strong as possible but the laughs still came through. Naturally, Milt got dressed to see who was laughing without him causing it. "They're talking about Joe Frisco," Walter Goldstein told Berle as he approached the Round Table. "Okay," Milton said, tapping one of the younger guys at the table, "get up and make room for players."

"You ain't heard nothin' yet," Milton started, stealing a Jolson line, "until you hear my favorite. When I first came to Hollywood, Joe greeted me at the Friars and said: 'This is the only t-town in the country wh-wh-where you wake up in the m-m-morning and listen to the b-birds coughing.'"

Naturally, Berle came up with an encore before the laugh died down: "Joe was working at Charlie Foy's place in those days and Charlie was complaining to his cast one night that he was suffering from thieves. 'I've just lost a whole chicken,' scowled Foy accusingly. 'D-D-Don't look at m-me,' Frisco called out, 'I didn't t-t-take it. If you don't believe it, w-w-weigh me!' "

You couldn't stop Berle now: "Once a Western Union boy who stuttered worse than Joe came to his room to take a telegram. 'G-G-Go back to the office,' Joe Frisco warned him, 'and tell them to s-s-send me a s-s-straight man.' "

A bylaw, written into the constitution of the club, is that the membership be two-thirds professional and one-third civilian or nonprofessional. The Round Table, however, is almost always professional and reserved for pros. It's the unwritten law of the Friars. Before you could say J-J-Joe F-F-Frisco, every seat was taken by a pro trying to get on.

Songwriters Jule Styne and Mitchell Parish and opera star Robert Merrill each came up with a Frisco story:

When Frisco was in the big money, he showed a genius for getting rid of it. His agent begged him, "Use your head, Joe, put away at least ten thousand a year, you'll never miss it, for the next ten years and you'll have a hundred grand in the bank. Then when the next depression hits us—you'll be sitting on top of the world." "F-F-Forget it," Joe growled. "With m-m-my luck, we won't have a next depression, and I'll be s-s-stuck with a h-h-hundred thousand bucks."

Robert Merrill said he was sitting with Frisco when a midget walked over unobserved, propped his chin on the edge of the table, and looked at Joe sadly. Joe took one look and screamed to the waiter, "Who ordered J-J-John the Baptist?"

The yarns about stutterin' Joe Frisco are part of the legend of our business. If another Frisco type came around in this Jet Age he'd be an anachronism. Joe Frisco was a man of those times. He could never have made it today. Today there are no places for the Friscos of the world to work.

Joe Frisco was the comedians' comedian. He was the court jester for the 14-karat, big-time funnymen who would spur their gag writers, press agents, and business managers during those same off-hours Frisco would spend at the track. Joe didn't work at his profession. He didn't work at improving himself. He was a character who just happened to make his living in show business. He didn't try to build up his equity or worry about percentage because what did he need? Most of his life he had no wife, never a big home with servants and cars and parties and upkeep. For Joe life was a single room and a scratch sheet. Joe Frisco had the spare time, the genius for blowing money, and the Runyonesque mentality it took to be a genuine "character," and everybody but his landladies loved him for it.

Even today there's rarely a gathering of variety buffs without someone coming up with a Joe Frisco story.

Peter Lind Hayes told us about when Joe entered the lobby of the Sherman Hotel in Chicago. The scrubwoman had shined up all the cuspidors and piled them in a corner in front of a large picture of maestro Abe Lyman posted there to advertise his coming appearance. "H-H-He's a great guy, that Lyman," praised Joe, "b-b-but he never won all those cups."

Julie Styne's favorite is the one about Bing Crosby, who was a loyal follower of the little guy with the cigar and the scratch sheets. Crosby had been lending Joe one $20 bill after another to go to the races, and Joe didn't pay them back. Finally, at Santa Anita, Joe got on a long shot and won a bundle. He began treating everybody at the bar and soon a mob was around him. Bing came up and from the outer fringe of the crowd he called to the celebrity, "Hey, Frisco, how about me?" Joe grandiosely peeled off a twenty and said to Crosby, "H-H-Here boy, sing two ch-ch-choruses of 'Melancholy Baby.'"

The genius who composed such classics as "Star Dust," "Deep Purple," "Sophisticated Lady," and "Take Me in Your Arms" is a pushover for any Frisco tale. Mitchell Parish tells of the time Joe was at the height of his career and was called down to the Income Tax Bureau for neglecting to pay $12,000 in taxes. "I h-h-h-haven't g-g-got it right now," Joe apologized. "The horses t-t-took it, but I'm g-g-good for it. K-K-Keep in touch with me." Luckily the inspector was a fan. "Listen, Mr. Frisco," he pleaded, "pay us a little every week and we'll straighten it out." Joe promised to be a good boy. As he stepped away from the desk, he noticed that Pat Rooney, Jr., was called next. It seems that Rooney, of the famous dancing family, owed about $900. Frisco walked back to the desk, put his arm around the youngest of the Rooneys, and said to the income-tax man, "This is a g-g-great little k-k-kid. I know his whole f-f-family. Put his b-b-bill on my tab."

Dais left to right, *Morey Amsterdam, Eddie Cantor, Myron Cohen, Abel Green, Harry Hershfield, Frank Sinatra, Milton Berle, George Jessel, Phil Silvers, Earl Wilson, and Mike Todd.*

5

The X-Rated Luncheons

In this era of masochistic comedy our most famous personalities have accepted testimonials just to be cut up by their friends. Ever since Maurice Chevalier became the first target of the dais assassins in 1949, the Friars have lived by the motto: "I come to bury him—not to praise him." In one recent killing it was Howard Cosell.

The idea is—if you think of something nice about the guy—forget it. If you have something nasty—let's hear it. Nobody ever unintentionally insults anybody at these luncheons—it's premeditated murder.

And it's got to be X-rated. Pity the poor comic. He has to clean it all up for TV—and dirty it up for the Friars roast. If *I bleep* out the words, I'm sure you'll understand.

When the Friars decided to dishonor Howard Cosell at a stag luncheon, 1,800 bloodthirsty souls showed up at the Americana Hotel for the lynching. It was coincidental with the premier of his new book about his life. No, it wasn't *Jaws*.

Milton Berle was the head executioner. His opening line was: "Let me tell you about Cosell. Never has a man been more sworn at—more spit at—more maligned—and rightfully so!" Then he added, "Isn't it amazing what with the problems of the world, inflation, wars all over, Watergate, that we stop everything to give a luncheon to a loudmouthed *bleep* like this *bleeping bleep*.

"Today, paying homage to Howard Cosell is like naming Bella Abzug the *bleep* of the month.

"Of course, we don't want Mr. Cosell to get too emotional because we're doing this luncheon for him. Being in the Friars is like having hemorrhoids—sooner or later every ass gets one.

"We don't want to make this afternoon too long, Howard has to get home because this is the night he gets his annual urge—and his wife gets her annual headache.

"I read his book *Cosell by Cosell* and it's a lot of bull*bleep*. I did some research and I'll tell you the real story. Howard came from a poor but stupid family. He is of Jewish extraction—he once pulled out of an Israeli hooker named Shirley. Howard was born at home—but when his mother saw him she went to the hospital. The neighborhood the Cosells lived in was so run down they didn't have toilets—just pay bushes.

"The Cosells lived in a neighborhood so tough, Abe Rellis was the Avon lady. When success came to Howard he couldn't handle it. He became so in love with himself—he had his thing monogrammed.

"And then true love came into his life, he met the lady—his lovely wife Marie Edith. Howard proposed and he said: 'I'm saving myself for you, darling. There isn't anyone else, is there?' And she said, 'Holy Christ, there must be!' And on their honeymoon night she said, 'Aren't you going to make love to me?' And he said, 'I can't, it's Lent,' and she said, 'You schmuck, why don't you borrow another one?'

"In the early 1950s he wanted to become a Friar. I was the abbot and I didn't want to sponsor the bastard. I finally said, 'Look, Howard, we've already got one putz in the club,' and Cosell said, 'I know—but suppose he gets sick?'"

Berle next introduced Georgie Jessel: "I've known him a lifetime. One of the all-time great orators—old silver tongue, as he's known to thousands of women who never heard him speak.

"Sitting next to him, talking to him, he's not as senile as you might think for his age—of course, he is putting on a little mileage. He's got the only piece of meat that hasn't gone up this month—and now the most decorated civilian in America, the toastmaster general, Georgie Jessel."

A Jessel highlight was: "I am here to honor Howard Cosell, a fine man who I've known—oh, for about fifteen minutes. But I know a story about him that's true. He had terrible pains and was told to take acupuncture—well, he said, 'I'm a little afraid of it'—so in order to get him in the mood for acupuncture—he screwed a porcupine."

Comedian Joe Morrow was next: "I can't tell you how nervous I am up here. Not only as an entertainer but as an avid sports fan who has enjoyed Howard Cosell. When his book came out I read it. I won't *horsebleep* you, I read the book. Word by word, sentence by

Dean Buddy Howe presents Frank with the Friars Abbot. The roast was well done by Howard Cosell, William B. Williams, Robert Merrill, Milton Berle, Cary Grant, and David Tebet.

sentence, paragraph by paragraph, and I'm now in the process of wiping my behind with it page by page."

Somebody from the Jets got up to talk about Cosell: "When he was playing football, this schmuck thought the best way to stop an end run was to use Preparation H."

I also had a few unkind words to say about the guest of honor: "I've known him man and boy for forty-six years—and I don't like him any more as a man than I did as a boy—one thing you can say about Howard Cosell—success hasn't changed him—he's still the same arrogant *bleep-heel* he always was.

"I would like to say something nice about this *bleep* but I just can't think of it. I would bring you a present, Howard, but what do you give a guy who has nothing? One thing you can be sure—there's never a dull moment when Cosell is on the air—it lasts the entire show. Lots of people owe a lot to him. Ulcers, nausea, diarrhea. Cosell has become a household word—garbage is also a household word. But don't sell him short. In college he was a four-letter man and they called him *bleep*."

Joey Russell said: "I heard you're a big *bleep*—so how come you're such a lousy lover, like Milton and everybody says. If you had between your legs what you got between your eyes—you'd be a big hero.

Executive Director Walter Goldstein giving the X-rating to Don Rickles, Norm Crosby, and George Raft at the Raft roast.

A *Friars roast with Pearl Bailey, Henny Youngman, Arthur Godfrey, Perle Mesta, Cab Calloway, and Stanley Adams.*

"Howard and Muhammad Ali are great friends. And perhaps you may wonder why. Howard owns an apartment house in Cherry Hill and he gave an apartment to Ali. A few days later, he called him up and said, 'I'd like to coop your joint,' and he did—and they've been fast friends ever since."

Dick Capri's contribution: "I'm a bachelor, Mr. Cosell, I've been a bachelor for six or seven years. I do all my own cooking. I've made a lot of food in the last few years. I've baked a lot of liver, I broiled a lot of ribs, I've pickled some feet, but this is the first time I have ever had an opportunity to roast an ass."

Berle introduced Gene Baylos as "the man with a physical handicap—he's hard of spending. He's so cheap that the only time he'll pick up a check is when it's made out to him."

"*I'm* cheap?" Gene screamed. "*I'm* cheap? This *bleep* has his Trojans dry-cleaned—then he sells them to Cosell as chewing gum. I had dinner with Berle and Cosell at the Stage Deli and before either one of them picked up the check, the restaurant changed hands twice. But I'm your friend, Howard. Remember you were sick—the doctor gave you six months to live—didn't I offer to buy you a calendar? I don't need this lunch—at my age, cream of wheat is too *bleeping* spicy. But I came here to honor you as the man of the year—and you know what a bad *bleeping* year it's been."

The president of ABC Sports, Roone Arledge, was the next speaker. "You are tough company—you also run very late. Following Milton Berle is like getting a kidney transplant from a bed wetter. I came here to say a few words about what Howard Cosell is really like to work with. He's a pain in the *bleeping* ass is what he is—and the idea that this many people would turn out to kiss his ass is absurd. I will tell you very quickly how we think of Howard's performance on ABC. We like to think of his performance on the air as being a lot like masturbation—it's disgusting for people to watch—but he get's such a kick out of it—we just haven't been able to tell him to stop. Thank you!"

Jerry Shane said: "Howard definitely has the gift of gab, as you know. He was destined to be a broadcaster. Ever since he was a young man, Howard knew he'd be a member of a news team because he was always the anchor man at a gang bang."

Pat Henry was next: "I love Howard Cosell but I can't sit next to him. I got stoned sniffing the *bleeping* glue on his toupee. But I love Howard—very few people know this man was born an only twin. And to look at him you know that he wasn't a very good-looking baby. In fact, when the doctor held him up at birth, he slapped him in the *bleeping* face. When his mother saw him, she slapped the *bleeping* doctor in the face. Do you know until Howard was sixteen years old, the family was still trying for an abortion. I'm gonna tell you one secret before I go—that's not a toupee he's wearing—that's Xaviera Hollander's *bleep* he's wearing on his head."

Jackie Kahane was loving: "I'm glad Roone Arledge, the president of ABC Sports, is here. Now I know how Howard got bad breath—it wasn't from kissing Ronne's hand. Now what the hell

A Friars petition to Martin and Lewis together.

does he know about sports? Just because he once smelled Mrs. Knute Rockne's bicycle seat? As a young man, Howard was not popular in school. He'd be beat up every time, every day after school. But he was the only kid who'd give a play-by-play of the beatings. Howard Cosell is a Jew. His real name is Cohen. Howard isn't ashamed of the fact that he is Jewish. It's the Jews who are ashamed. Even though his wife is a Protestant and Howard is a Jew, they both believe in the same God—Howard. In conclusion I want to thank all Howard's friends here who chipped in $10,000 to have his dentist cap his mouth."

Milton introduced Henny Youngman as "the king of the one-liners—that's because the schmuck can't remember two. Youngman is the only comic in town that can tell four jokes in a minute, because he's never interrupted by laughs. I love him—I have no taste, but I love him. Here he is—the putz of the month—Henny Youngman."

Henny started on Milton first: "I've known Berle, man and woman, for forty years—and he's always been a *bleep*. Milton, Macy's called—your dresses are ready. Say, Howard, I've been looking high and low for you—but I guess I didn't look low enough. I'm here to talk about Howard Cosell. What do you say about a guy who gets up in the morning and shaves his tongue? Howard developed the flair for making money, even as a kid. What a smart idea—putting get-well cards into Kotex boxes. Before I leave I want to tell you one thing, Howard, next time you buy a toupee—get one with brains. And Milton, I have two words for you—*bleep you*."

Berle introduced the executive director, Walter Goldstein, who presented Cosell with a watch: "I'd like to say, Mr. Cosell, when the truly great names of the sports announcers are read—you'll be sitting there listening."

"Now," Milton said to Cosell, "stand up and defend yourself, you big *bleep—*"

"I don't know how so many of you have struggled through the disaster that's taking place," Howard answered. "We began approximately six hours ago and if ever there was a vivid evidence of why vaudeville is dead—you've witnessed it today.

"Truly it's been a glorious occasion for me—circumscribed almost as always by absolute mediocrity—but thank God you've had the opportunity at long last to honor the greatest mouth of his time—thank you all very much."

After a century of listening and participating in dozens of X-rated luncheons, you forget who did what to whom and who got paid for what and who meant it. I only know the knife is always out, as well as the dirt. Wasn't it Oscar Wilde who said: "You always hurt the ones you love"—or was it Gene Baylos?

Johnny Carson said at the roast for Alan King: "All I've been reading about in the papers for the last three weeks is our guest of honor—and I'm tired of it. 'Alan King has twelve television guest shots'—'Alan King has his own situation comedy'—'Alan King is producing four shows'—'Alan King has the old Rodgers and Hammerstein estate in Great Neck'—'Alan King has a Rolls-Royce.' Just one morning I'd like to pick up the paper and see—'Alan King has Gonorrhea.'"

50

Then he said, before they closed the lid, "It's not that I'm jealous of Alan—he's got a lovely family—he's got success—he's got a lovely home—he's got his own show—and he'd give it all up in a minute for one thing—talent."

Phil Silvers said: "Alan has everything—money—fame—youth—good looks—a vest, a Rolls-Royce—and in spite of all that he doesn't cheat or fool with broads—so I want you to know that you came out in this inclement weather to honor a real schmuck."

Corbett Monica said he was in England where Alan is a big favorite: "He's played TV and theatres in London and even did half a dozen command performances. That means they love him there. Either that or he's *bleeping* the queen."

At the Joey Bishop vivisection Red Buttons interjected the first needle: "When the iceman cometh—I hope he cometh all over you."

Don Rickles was kind to Joey: "I hope you jump on a bicycle and discover it has no seat."

Harry Hershfield said: "I watch all these young comedians like Joey Bishop—I'm three times his age—and my position is like the dog who had his *bleep* cut off. But he kept running around with the other dogs. So they said to him, 'What are you running around

Marilyn Monroe and friends Eddie Fisher and Sam Levinson at the Martin and Lewis roast.

From left to right, *Jack E. Leonard, Milton Berle, Rocky Marciano, Pat O'Brien,* and *Perry Como, at the Rocky Marciano luncheon at the Park Sheraton Hotel on October 30, 1952.*

with us for?—your *bleep* was cut off,' and he says, 'I'm now a consultant.'

"Now a word about the Friars. The spirit of the Friars. It's like the two fellas on the street having an argument as two women walk by. One guy said to the other '*bleep* you' and one woman turns to the other and says, 'Did you ever hear that word before?' She says, 'Yes—but never in anger.'"

At the Milton Berle murder, Al Bernie said respectfully, "Unfortunately I am not as intimate with Milton Berle as others. But I know that beneath his egotism, underneath that brashness—he's a no-good son of a bitch.

"Now take Bob Hope, for example. Take away his class, his dignity, his charm, and what have you got? Milton Berle!"

Red Buttons said: "Berle is now an author. His writing leaves you with a distinctive flavor—horse*bleep*. He had a coauthor because he didn't want to take the rap alone."

Milton replied: "To all of you I say, 'Up your *bleep*.' I want you to know that I'm honored at the wonderful room full of stars—but no matter how many of these wonderful parties you may give me, I will *not* get out of show business."

Jack E. Leonard said at the Joe E. Lewis party: "Joe E. uses all the facilities at the Friars. Goes to our gym and gets a rubdown every day only because the alcohol is a hundred proof—"

Jack Barry said: "All those stories about Joe E. drinking and sinning are exaggerated. As a matter of fact, I find it hard to believe a woman could satisfy Joe. I mean I can't believe any woman could satisfy Joe after he's been *bleeped* so often by touts and horses."

I said: "I'm here to honor Joe E.—the flask with a head on it. This is the idol of millions? Years ago we used to look up to men like Horatio Alger, Babe Ruth for his clean living, Johnny Weissmuller for his swinging through the air gracefully. Today our idol is a degenerate, drunken whoremaster. Everybody loves him, like they do the TV stars.

"They say, look at Ed Sullivan—isn't he wonderful—he doesn't smile. Isn't Steve Allen wonderful—he has no personality. Look at Jack Paar. Isn't he marvelous—he's a putz. Now they revere Joe E.—isn't he wonderful—he's a drunk. Isn't he great?—he lost his wife on a crap table. Isn't he magnificent?—he pays $50 for a $10 broad. What magnificent?—he's a bum.'"

The Jerry Lewis party brought out all the sharpshooters: Jan Murray hollered: "This *bleeping bleep* is 'Man of the Year'? I wouldn't vote him 'Jew of the Block.'" Johnny Carson noted: "Jerry is a unique individual—he's the only man in the world belted in the mouth by Mahatma Gandhi."

Jack Carter said: "Jerry is a charitable man—last year an old-age home came to see him and he gave them a tremendous donation—his mother and father." Milton Berle: "Jerry is the only man to get a Dear John letter from Typhoid Mary—they caught him selling Portnoy coloring books on Sesame Street." Charlie Callas said: "In France Jerry Lewis is hailed as a genius. That's the same country that burned Joan of Arc."

Morey Amsterdam said: "Jerry likes to sing—he does all the Jolson songs. Now he is imitating Bing Crosby singing 'Love Thy Neighbor' and started more wife swapping than any time in history."

The Jack Carter roast was sweet. Dave Barry said: "Jack is the Muhammad Ali of bull*bleep*." Milton Berle said: "Jack Carter is the only man in America who could go to Denmark for an operation—and still come back a big putz. Another thing about Jack, he's a real religious Jew. In Las Vegas last Yom Kippur he didn't *bleep* one chorus girl."

Red Buttons said: "Jack Carter was the model for those kosher salamis—after Milton Berle turned it down." Milton hollered: "I didn't turn it down—I couldn't get it up."

6

The Round Table

The Round Table at the Friars, like the Lambs Club, the Algonquin, the Players Club, or Hillcrest, came into its own so that an actor could have another platform to talk about himself.

One reason an actor likes a Broadway play is so he can complain to the guys at the Round Table that he's weary of working. He likes to go on the road so he can complain he misses Broadway. He likes to make a movie so he can complain about Hollywood. What he really likes is to get "on"—and only about himself. You can always pick out actors by the glazed look they get when the conversation wanders away from them.

An actor would rather have a seat at the Round Table at the Friars, Algonquin, the Players, Lambs, or Hillcrest than a seat on the stock exchange. That's why the table is round. If it were square or oblong, somebody would have to be at its head and nobody wants second billing. The Round Table is an equalizer. Everybody shines equally from Gene Baylos to Bob Hope, from George Burns to Henny Youngman.

Me, I love show people—especially comedians. I love them for their illusions as much as for their talents, their exaggerations, their persistency, their guts, their faith in God and themselves—and I hope, in this case, they forgive me for giving God top billing.

When a biggie—one whose background is primarily vaudeville—arrives in town to plug a movie, a TV show, or a book, the clan meets early to get a seat at the Round Table, because they know the Friars is going to be jumping.

George Burns was "on" recently when I showed up one day. He was talking about his new movie *The Sunshine Boys*, naturally: "The last picture I did was in 1939 for MGM," George was saying, "and it was called *Honolulu*. I must have made a good impression because here it is only thirty-six years later and they brought me back."

Milton Berle interrupted, which is not easy when Burns is on. "Now that you're a movie star again, I hear the broads swoon at you." "I got very faithful fans," answered the eighty-year-old Burns, "but when they swoon now, it takes them longer to get up."

George Burns, like many old-time comedians, started his career on the sidewalks of New York. He was seven when he was a member of the Peewee Quartet singing on street corners, in saloons, and small-time vaudeville. He still would rather sing than throw jokes. He met Gracie Allen at Union Station and started their act in 1922. Gracie was the straight man and he had the comedy lines. However, when he saw that the audiences weren't getting laugh cramps at his gravel-voiced smart-ass answers but, instead, were doubling up at her questions, he changed the act. He played the straight and Gracie became the comedian. They were married four years later during a three-day layoff in Detroit (1925) and so the immortal team of Burns and Allen was born.

Now Georgie is alone and like so many other loners he loves to join the boys at the Round Table talking about what agent screwed what act, who stole whose material, which star is making it with which chorine, and other such important problems of state.

"Why don't you retire?" Georgie asked Berle at this session, "you've been a star a long time." Berle answered, "I'm ten years younger than you are, why don't *you* retire?" Burns counterpunched, "I can't quit now—I'm all booked up." Milton said, "How can *I* quit? I still have 300 glossy pictures and $200 worth of makeup left."

The Round Table idea started in the 1920s at the Algonquin Hotel on West 44th Street. Different than the Friars or Lambs, they encouraged women to join their select circle, the ground rules being that no special attentions were paid to them just because they used the ladies' room. When a female pulled out a chair at the Round Table, no male stood up for her or offered any masculine courtesies. It was expected that she'd be treated as one of the boys. Any lunchtime you could find some of the sharpest minds and pens of literature and the theatre throwing their rehearsed ad-libs at each other: George S. Kaufman, Alexander Woollcott, Dorothy Parker, Ring Lardner, were a few of the headliners with frequent guest appearances by Tallulah, Harpo, Noel, Edna Ferber, and Robert E. Sherwood among others.

In 1920, when Frank Case, who owned the Algonquin Hotel, shoved a large round table into the hotel's Rose Room for the purpose of catering to a gaggle of the young unknown literati, he never thought he was making history. How could he ever dream that someday this would be dubbed "The Round Table" and would boast of such knights as Alfred Lunt and Lynn Fontanne, Charles MacArthur, Franklin P. Adams, Robert Benchley, and Heywood Broun who, massed together, formed a jury that they themselves referred to as the "Vicious Circle." Some of America's greatest one-liners were born at the famed Round Table of the Algonquin Hotel:

Alexander Woollcott, called by one critic "the worst writer in America," told the gang: "I'm potentially the best writer in America, but I never had anything to say." Robert Benchley, probably one of the greatest comedy writers of all time, always denigrated himself publicly: "It took me fifteen years to discover I had no talent for writing, but I couldn't give it up because by that time I was too famous."

Franklin Pierce Adams, whom everybody referred to as F.P.A., was regarded as the father of the Round Table. His column, "The Conning Tower," went on for thirty years or more and showed up in three New York newspapers: The *Herald Tribune*, the *World*, and the *Post*. He was acting executioner of the vicious circle. When George Bernard Shaw went on record as saying that schoolteachers ought to have babies, F.P.A. said, "Well, he ought to know; he's had schoolteachers." When Alexander Woollcott signed a first-edition copy of his book *Shouts and Murmurs*, Woollcott sighed, "Oh, what is so rare as a Woollcott first edition?" And F.P.A. zinged, "A Woolcott second edition." When the name of one disliked member was brought up, somebody said, "He's his own worst enemy," and F.P.A. interjected, "Not while I'm around."

Onetime drama critic Robert Benchley, who was well aware of his lack of responsibility where finances were concerned, applied for a loan at his corner bank. To his surprise the money was granted without any questions asked. The next day he withdrew all his savings explaining to his cronies at the Round Table, "I don't trust a bank that would lend money to such a poor risk."

Acid-tongued Benchley about a Broadway show he had just

reviewed: "It was one of those plays in which all the actors unfortunately enunciated very clearly."

Benchley about fellow Round Tabler Dorothy Parker with whom he temporarily shared a tiny $30-a-month office: "One cubic foot less of space, and it would have constituted adultery."

Benchley about a famous Hollywood movie queen who had just died and whose sex life had been noted in gossip columns from Long Beach, Long Island, to Long Beach, California: "She sleeps alone at last."

Columnist and crusader Heywood Broun could have been the most lethal of the circle: He once carved up a liberal as "a man who leaves the room when the fight starts." Broun reported to the Round Table in 1935: "Nobody need worry anymore that Washington is going left. Indeed, nobody need worry that the Washington of today is going anywhere."

It was after a minor operation that Heywood composed a lyric for his surgeon, which he submitted to the Round Table:

> There was a young man with a hernia
> Who said to his surgeon, "Gol-dernya,
> When carving my middle
> Be sure you don't fiddle
> With matters that do not concernya."

George S. Kaufman, often called the "gloomy dean of American humor," was the author of some forty or more plays and musical comedies. As a young theatre critic he won admission to the Algonquin Round Table when he was assigned to cover a new Broadway comedy and in his homicidal review administered this death blow: "There was laughter in the back of the theatre, leading to the belief that somebody was telling jokes back there." He won a permanent high chair in the vicious circle when he said of the show *Skylark* starring Gertrude Lawrence: "It was a bad play saved by a bad performance."

Ring Lardner, another predator, was considered to be America's master of the short story. Once a pompous hippie-type with a long flowing mane approached him at the Table. "How do you look when I'm sober?" Ring asked the intruder.

Dorothy Parker was a literary critic, short story and verse writer, and like most of her fellow-tablers a dramatic critic whose mouth could be declared a lethal weapon. Reporting on a Yale prom,

Miss Parker swooped, "If all those sweet young things present were laid end to end, I wouldn't be at all surprised."

Describing a guest at one of her parties: "That woman speaks eighteen languages and can't say 'no' in any of them." When it was announced at the Table that Calvin Coolidge was dead, she asked, "How can you tell?"

One of the Rounders asked her if she enjoyed a certain cocktail party. "Enjoyed it? One more drink and I'd have been under the host," she replied. On being shown a swank Manhattan apartment, Dorothy complained to the real-estate agent, "Oh dear, that's much too big. All I need is room enough to lay a hat and a few friends."

Alexander Woollcott's line, uttered a rainy Thursday at the Round Table, has become a classic of American wit: "All the things I really like to do are either immoral, illegal, or fattening." And it was Edna Ferber who is quoted as mothering this one: "Being an old maid is like death by drowning, a really delightful sensation after you cease to struggle."

The cast of the Algonquin Round Table changes over the years but the taste for blood lingers on. It's the same at the Lambs, the Friars, and the Hillcrest Country Club in Beverly Hills. The famed Hillcrest has attracted some of the biggest to its luncheon Round Table. Unfortunately, the average age of its members is deceased. For instance, George Burns has lunch there every day with such veterans as Georgie Jessel and Lou Holtz who like to wheeze by to cut up a few touches and a few cohorts.

My keenest recollection of Hillcrest was when the venerable movie mogul Adolph Zukor celebrated his one hundredth birthday. It was quite a party. The last to arrive, Jack Benny, warmly congratulated the centenarian and Mr. Zukor peered up at the eighty-year-old Benny and asked, "Are you still around?"

The Lambs Round Table has survived fires, attacks, as well as bankruptcies. Even now the same table is secure and surrounded by the greatest names in the theatre in its new home at 5 East 66th Street sharing the facilities of the Lotus Club.

The same table has been decorated with everybody from Adolph Zukor, Smith and Dale, Edwin Booth, the Barrymores, and illustrious shepherds like Bert Lytell, William Greaza, William Gaxton and, of course, the beloved Harry Hershfield.

It wasn't unusual to see Jack Dempsey, the "can you top this" gang, Harry Hershfield, Joe Laurie, Jr., Senator Ford, and Peter

The Round Table at the Copa. From left to right, owner Jules Podell, Danny Thomas, Mrs. Ted Lewis, Eve Sully, Ida Cantor, Jesse Block, Eddie Cantor, and Mr. and Mrs. Jimmy Durante.

Donald, sitting with Bert Lahr, Douglas Fairbanks, Jr., Frank Fay, and Bert Wheeler cutting up pieces of cake and each other. Imagine Bobby Clark, Jack Waldron, Pat O'Brien, John Charles Thomas, Jack Pearl, and Jackie Gleason throwing lines at each other at one session.

The Lambs Round Table started in London about 1840. In those far-off days the home of Charles Lamb, essayist, critic, and leader in London's literary life, was a rendezvous for luminaries in the world of arts and letters. Charles Lamb and his sister Mary maintained a continuing and generous open house with all the drinks and eats on the house, of course. Every actor in town suggested, after their shows, "Let's go 'round to the Lambs!" That became a habit until this day. Maybe that's why they went bankrupt. They still expected everything "on the house."

When the Lambs came to New York in 1874, it was an era of horsecars, bustles, and whiskey "at five cents the glass." When theatrical life centered around Union Square. Nearby on 14th Street, Delmonico's popular restaurant was a landmark. On Broadway, a block below stood Wallacks' Theatre. The first Round Table was in the Blue Room of Delmonico's and they have been going uptown by degrees since—to 16th Street, to 36th Street, 44th Street, and now 66th Street.

The Lambs new young shepherd, Tom Dillon, and I were sitting around his table. Through the years the usage has ripened into tradition and today's fledgling is aware that the Round Table is "off limits" except through invitation. Tom and I remembered some of the "invited" guests who made history around the table:

Frank Fay was a brilliant comic who was a self-made man and adored his maker. "I insist I'm not conceited," he said often, "although you realize I have every right to be." Bert Wheeler chided him one lunchtime, "I agree you're great but how could you stand up in court and say you're the greatest living actor of all time?" Fay pulled himself up to his full ego and answered, "I was under oath—I didn't want to commit perjury."

One bum approached the great John Barrymore and pleaded for a quarter for something to eat. The disciple of the bard looked down at him and in his full Shakespearean manner said, "Young man, 'Neither a lender nor a borrower be'—William Shakespeare." The bum looked up and said, " 'Screw you'—Tennessee Williams."

It seems a couple of hoofers finally made it into vaudeville's mecca, New York's Palace Theatre. Entering the Lambs Club, they saw Wilton Lackaye, who was headlining the bill in a dramatic sketch, drinking in the corner by himself. Trepidatiously, one of the hoofers walked over and said, "Mr. Lackaye, we're so proud to be on the same bill with you and to know we are fellow Lambs. It would make us happy if you'd let us buy you a drink." "I'm sorry," Lackaye answered, "but you see, I've just lost my mother and I'd rather be alone right now." "I know exactly how you feel," said the hoofer full of sympathy, "we lost our trunk."

Tom Dillon was sitting with William Gaxton, Fred Astaire, Jim Barton, and Rube Goldberg when this producer came by and announced to all, "I think I got a hit." Tom asked, "How do you know?" The big man answered, "I met three of the critics and they each told me that if I change one of the acts, I'll have a hit." "Say," said Astaire, "that's wonderful." "Yeah, but each picked a different act."

As shepherd of the Lambs, Harry Hershfield led his flock through a lifetime of laughs. It was typical of "Mr. New York," who had a quip for every occasion, that shortly before he died at the age of eighty-nine he said at the Round Table: "My song is over—but my malady lingers on."

When I told Harry that Tom Jones says he lives his life like each day is his last day on earth, Harry answered, "I live my life like every day is my first day on earth."

All the Lambs suggested that he take it easy and Hershfield answered, "I'd collapse—but I'm too weak." Harry had all kinds of advice for his table mates: "A conscience cannot prevent sin; it only prevents you from enjoying it." Another time he said, "New York is a city where everyone mutinies but no one deserts." Naturally, he even joked about his own death. He said his epitaph should read: "Here lies the body of Harry Hershfield. If not, notify Ginsberg and Co., undertakers, at once."

In the old days the primary school for young comics, before they graduated to the Lambs, Hillcrest, or the Friars, was Hanson's drugstore on 51st Street and 7th Avenue. The Round Table there was the lunch counter otherwise known as "The Corn Exchange." Any noontime you could find Jack E. Leonard, Jack Carter, Lenny Bruce, Jerry Lewis, Buddy Hackett, Jan Murray, Dean Martin, Red Buttons, Phil Foster, and dozens of other young comedians swapping lies and material.

Hanson's was wall-to-wall show biz. Sure, you could get your prescriptions filled or pick up a Dr. Scholl's foot plaster, bottle of aspirin or any of the other products the usual corner drugstore would stock. But this corner was different because it was within one block of everything—the Winter Garden Theatre, the Capitol Theatre, the Mark Hellinger Theatre, Radio City Music Hall—and Hanson's was a theatrical emporium. Its customers were chorus girls and chorus boys and its goodies were toupee glue, the kind of false lashes you can see from the third balcony, Mehron's greasepaint, lip gloss, panchromatic makeup, rabbits' feet for applying rouge, Johnson & Johnson's liquid adhesive which when dry changes the shape of your nose or face, stick-on nails, paste-on eyebrows, and the other etceteras of the trade.

In addition, Hanson's was a supermarket for gags and social director material. There you could swap two Milton Berle parodies for one Red Skelton Guzzler's Gin routine or twelve Bob Hope jokes for a Willie Howard sketch. If you had a good Richy Craig, Jr., opening routine or a couple of only slightly used Lou Holtz stories, you could pick up some practically brand-new scenes or three-quarters of a pantomime record bit or maybe even a whole act recently introduced by Joe E. Lewis out of writer Eli Basse.

I was a big man on the exchange because I had such blue-chip trading stock as the best of Jackie Osterman, Lou Holtz, Frank Fay, and a socko six minutes of Milton Berle, all of which had cost me a fortune in matinee tickets at the Regent, Alhambra, Palace, and Loew's State theatres. But what the traders considered really gilt-edged negotiables were my Georgie Jessel routines. These I had personally copied down after spending three days without food or water watching Georgie at the Roxy. When I auctioned off his "Mamma on the Telephone," I did the routine for my customers exactly as Jessel did it. This raised its value even higher. The telephone bit, with specific instructions as to how to deliver each punch line, netted me twenty dialect jokes and one "surefire, only slightly used monologue."

"I'll never forget the battle at Hanson's Round Table when Gene Baylos grabbed Lenny Bruce and yelled, "You bum, you stole my Bob Hope routine."

One block away from Hanson's was Lindy's. The famous old Lindy's restaurant. It was there among the smoked tongues that the real live hams got their training in the art of sadistic humor.

The idea was, "If you can't say anything nice about the guy—let's hear it." This subsequently evolved into the theme of the Friars roast, which prides itself on the massacre of the honored guest.

Lindy's on the northwest corner of 51st Street and Broadway was the heart and the stomach of the variety world. The arteries radiating in every direction from Lindy's—uptown, downtown, crosstown, 7th Avenue, Broadway, 50th Street, 49th Street, 52nd Street—were ablaze with neon signs and marquee lights. Any week you could catch maybe a Guy Lombardo and His Royal Canadians plus Jane Powell across the street at the Capitol Theatre while at the same time Frank Sinatra was doing his thing at the Paramount Theatre while Milton Berle and a cast of thousands were a block down at the Roxy.

And crisscrossing every avenue on every street were the legitimate theatres winking and blinking with names like Ethel Merman, Bert Lahr, Mary Martin, Ray Bolger, Bea Lillie, Gertrude Lawrence, Al Jolson. Catercorner down the road apiece could have been Judy Garland at the Palace or, almost every time you looked up, Sophie Tucker at Lou Walters's Latin Quarter, and at one time or another the street Walter Winchell dubbed the Great Watt Way and Mazda Lane sparkled with imports like maybe a Betty Grable, a Peter Lawford, a Dorothy Lamour who would be twinkling onstage at the Strand or Loew's State to push whatever the companion movie was the studios were desperate to push.

At the Taft Hotel, also across the street, we had Vincent Lopez and his orchestra. At the nearby Astor Hotel we might have had a Woody Herman and, if not, then a Jimmy or Tommy Dorsey, a Louis Armstrong, Benny Goodman, or Harry James. And if it wasn't these guys, then it was somebody else close to them because the Astor Roof always had gala balls and noisy proms and dancing to big-name bands.

That corner of the town at night was filled with glitter and glamour. The Round Table at Lindy's wasn't round and it wasn't always in the same place. Lindy's came alive after midnight. It's where the big shots and the small shots dropped by to have their snacks and take their bows after their shows. The floating round table was where the biggest star happened to be sitting at whatever front-section table happened to be available at whatever moment he happened to arrive with however many "gophers" and hangers-on were trailing along in his wake.

Wherever the stars congregate the columnists are sure to follow. This little zoo was feeding time for the newspaper guys who could make or break your heart in those days. The town boasted such pros as Danton Walker, Ed Sullivan, and Bob Sylvester of the New York *Daily News*, Louis Sobol and Dorothy Kilgallen of the New York *Journal American*, Hy Gardner of the *Herald Tribune*, Frank Farrell of the New York *World Telegram*, Earl Wilson and Leonard Lyons of the New York *Post*, Nick Kenny, Lee Mortimer, and Winchell of the New York *Daily Mirror*. Wherever one of those kings held court was another nucleus of the floating Round Table.

I was sitting near the entrance of Lindy's one late night with Morey Amsterdam. We were sharing a piece of what is immortalized in *Guys and Dolls* as "Mindy's cheesecake" and we were talking about Berle. "He's the greatest," Morey was saying, "but he doesn't hear you—he doesn't listen—unless he's stealing jokes." Just as we were saying this, the Master Himself sauntered over from his dressing room across the street where he had just finished his last show of the day. When Milton spied us he put his hand on my shoulder and greeted us, "Hi fellas—what's new? Five shows a day. I'm beat. I really killed 'em today. What fantastic audiences. How you doing?"—never waiting for an answer. Meanwhile, his hand was still clamped on my shoulder as he looked around to see if there was a more important star or newspaperman in the joint. Naturally, he didn't want to leave us yet because at the moment we were the heaviest names in the place and maybe this would end up being the Round Table.

"How are things, Morey?" Milton asked, not really listening for the answer, all the time his eyes darting around for a Winchell or Sullivan or, at the very least, a Bob Hope. Morey, knowing Milton didn't hear him, gave him this: "Oh, my wife is very sick, my brother is in the hospital, I was hit by a car, and my kid ran away from home." Continuing to pat my shoulder, Milton said, "Great, kid, great—glad to hear it." We won Milton that night and that night he became the abbot of our Round Table.

Another of Walter Winchell's regular nightly stops was the Stork Club. There he only granted audience to the big stars. In Lindy's he received all the press agents and lesser names who worshiped at his column. I still don't know how Walter got his news. He was always on and listened even less than Berle. Winchell was the High Executioner of the Fourth Estate. If he didn't like you or you gave him a wrong item, you might as well get out of the business. He would keep shooting at you until you were dead. A couple of decades ago he announced on the air and in his column that Bette Davis had an incurable disease and was dying. When Miss Davis denied it, press agent Jack Tierman said, "If Winchell says she's dying, she better be dying or she's in big trouble."

The Lindy's crowd were mesmerized into believing W.W. could make or break you with one item. I remember when he murdered a regular in his column without using his name. The guy threatened to sue. "But," his friends argued, "he didn't mention your name." "That's it," he hollered, "nobody'll know it's me!"

When you sat around Winchell's Round Table he insisted that you come right out and say what you think—if you agreed with him. Somebody said about W.W.: "He'll never change his religion—he thinks he's God." One late night Walter was sitting with a group of press agents talking about himself, of course, when I joined the table. Always glad to get another pair of ears he continued, "What do you think about that Truman—who the hell does he think he is? All the other presidents did what I told them. This one thinks he's bigger than Winchell. We had a lulu of an argument yesterday and he hasn't called me to at least say he's sorry."

I interrupted, but then anytime you were talking you were interrupting Winchell. I said, "Walter, why don't you call *him*, he's a pretty busy man—he's the president of the United States of America —he's got a big country to run."

"*He's* busy?" he screamed, "*he's* busy? Does he have six columns and a radio show to get out every week?"

Lindy's was the late night extension of the lunchtime Friars Round Table. As it got later and later at night even Lindy's subcontracted and laid off its somnambulists on other places like Reubens where we all had sandwiches named after us (mine was an impersonal blend of turkey and ham) or the Copa Lounge where disc jockey Jack Eigen would interview us or the Stage Delicatessen where the owner would interview us.

At the Stage Delicatessen the Big Star was the little chubby owner Max Asnas who talked with an accent so thick that many of his comments sounded like Sanskrit to the uninitiated. The sage of the Stage dispensed his Kosher philosophy at the drop of a bagel: "I vas born poor and I'll die poor," he recited in his own Castilian Yiddish, "in between, I'd like to be rich."

Jan Murray plopped down at Max's oblong Round Table one night and shouted, "Hey, foreigner, make me a pastrami sandwich." Max looked at Jan coolly and asked, "Your father and mother was Indians?"

Phil Silvers complained that he loved the Stage food and all but there was no place to park. "Why the hell haven't you got a parking lot for your customers?" Max reasoned: "If I had a parking lot—I wouldn't need a delicatessen."

Max was the ringmaster. His whole delicatessen was a stage, and pros of every size, shape, and salary, from Groucho to Paar, learned not to "start opp." When it comes to a punch line, M. Asnas, prop., left no customer unturned. Fat Jack E. Leonard yelled, "One of your clumsy waiters spilled mustard on my coat! This is an expensive coat." Max answered calmly, "You think this is cheap mustard?"

Fred Allen smiled at the boss when he stopped at his table. "Your food is very good," he complimented, "but it gave me heartburn." Max snapped, "So what do you expect in a delicatessen—sunburn?"

7

The Unwritten Law

There is an unwritten law in the Friars that actors, performers, musicians, and/or writers cannot approach agents, producers, directors and/or managers for jobs or auditions. I think the geniuses who wrote this unwritten law should know that it's not worth the paper it's not written on.

The big-shot talent buyers and sellers such as Buddy Howe, Lew Wasserman, Abe Lastvogel, Jimmy Nederlander, Nat Lefkowitz, Willard Alexander, Howard Minsky, Jackie Green, Larry Bennett, Milton Rackmill, and others who hide in their offices from actors find it pretty difficult to hide from them in the steam room with their faces and everything else hanging out. It's tough to look down on an actor when the actor can look down at you and find out you ain't exactly superior. I mean, go demonstrate superiority when you can't hide your inferiority behind a desk and you got no place to put your hands. The steam room is an equalizer.

Some of the biggest deals in show business were consummated in the sauna and steam rooms on the fifth floor. Take the case of Friar Norman King, the TV and radio promoter. He became a millionaire in the steam room. When he first joined the club he was broke and he lived in the sauna. The sauna was his home. The steam room his office. The only overhead he had was the towels and he had the phones and the beds for working and resting.

When William B. Williams proposed him for membership Norman was just starting in the media-buying service. His gimmick was telling people how to spend money on TV and radio and get more for their dollar. He invited prospects to the Friars; showed them how to live and how to spend—*their* money, of course—and he did it all in his office in the steam room. There everything was laid bare—everything was put on the table—and they bought it.

Some promoters use yachts and broads and stars to impress clients. Norman King used the steam room and became rich. Of course, his customers didn't know that this was all he had at the time—that it was his home and his office and his club.

That's one of the prime reasons the Friars will never allow females to become members. Ladies can come for dinner every night of the week. They can have brunch on Saturday afternoon. They can use the dining room on the main floor and the Joe E. Lewis and Milton Berle rooms on the second floor—but the third and fifth floors will always remain off limits. Special material writer Eli Basse grumbles, "The broads want in—but over my dead body." Which is probably the reason he doesn't want broads in..

"The wives of some of our members are dying to see who hangs out on the fifth floor steam room," Eli says. "May I truthfully say, girls, we all hang out on the fifth floor.

"However, ladies, if by law someday we are forced to admit women to become members, I warn you, you may be able to cope with the third floor where the card playing goes on or the fourth floor where the guys play pool—but on the fifth floor you'll never pass the physical."

Lou Holtz, the veteran vaudeville comic and dialectician, was always a faithful Friar. Once a friend asked, "How is it I never see you with a girl these days?" Holtz shrugged: "I spend my days in the Friars club and my evenings at home. If you want to see a ball game you gotta go to Yankee stadium, right? Same with girls. Neither the Friars nor my home is the place to see a ball game or meet girls."

Henny Youngman, who has more agents than the CIA, likes to meet them at the Friars without women around to distract from his one-liners. "That's why our stag lunches are so successful," Henny claims. "The obscenities even shocked Walter Cronkite, Ed Sullivan, and Tiny Tim. Imagine if women were allowed in!"

"Yeah, the Round Table would never be the same with broads around," Sol Violinsky used to say. "They get too dirty!" And then he added, "I want the luxury of a man's club. Give me the luxuries —anyone can have the necessities."

It's the wives of our members who are pushing for membership. Overcome with curiosity, they won't rest until they see what's going on on the third and fifth floors, until now untouched by human females. Some of the more suspicious wives believe our third floor is a private dining room with Xaviera Hollander as the maître d' and Linda Lovelace as the main dish.

"They say there must be something going on at the club," Eli says, "because there's nothing coming off at home. I think the wives of some of our members are confusing extracurricular activities with hardening of the arteries and hormone deficiencies. They don't know that one of our members developed a double hernia just by picking up a 400 spade hand."

The women's quest for equality has, however, infiltrated our sacred sanctum sanctorum. Just the fact that they have gained entry come nighttime, things are even different. After fifty years the lights in the hallowed halls are dimmed at dinner. Hallowed is an old Greek expression meaning falling apart. Some Greek philosopher once said—I think it was Joe DiMaggio or it could have been Joe E. Lewis: "Behind every man there's a women's liberation movement."

Joe E. warned every dean to "keep the broads out": "In ancient times women liberated themselves by poisoning their undesirable mates, a custom that is still going on in thousands of households where the gents are covered by insurance. This accounts for the fact that I take all my meals at the club. I'd rather be taken in than done in."

Joe, who never got up until five or six in the evening, then went straight to the bar because "I never eat on an empty stomach."

Old Doc Meylackson who has been the treasurer of the Friars for centuries is always ready to help every Friar in need and without charge. He walks around the room curing one and all. Meylackson is the only doctor in the world who makes table calls.

"I think it's ridiculous," Doc said, "that the wives of some of our members accuse us of sex discrimination. Fifty percent of our members have no sex at all—and the rest just like to talk about it."

When George Burns was in town he lamented his sex life with the Doc: "I'm only eighty but I can only have sex about once a month or so." "That's natural," said the Doc.

"Yeah," George complained, "but Groucho Marx is eighty-five and he says he has sex twice a week."

"Okay," said the Doc, "you say the same thing."

Sex is a sensitive subject at the Monastery. Lou Holtz was de-

Bill
Anderer

Inside the hallowed walls.

fending a friend of many years who was gay. "At his age," Lou explained, "he can only do it once a month—the entire act takes an hour—so for seven hundred and nineteen hours a month he is straight."

Every time Harry Hershfield sat down at the Round Table and they looked for a subject to discuss, Harry always said: "One thing we will not discuss and that's sex—what was *was*."

No matter how grandiose the Friars have become it's still a family affair. There is pride in being a member of a club that boasts such illustrious alumni as Mayor Jimmy Walker and President Woodrow Wilson. Woodrow Wilson joined after the Friars big Road Frolic of 1916, which played sixteen cities in fourteen days with a cast of George M. Cohan, Will Rogers, Willie Collier, Hedda Hopper's actor husband DeWolfe Hopper, Irving Berlin, Julian Eltinge, Lew Dockstader, and Victor Herbert and his orchestra.

The finale was a hilarious takeoff on the cause célèbre of the day, the rootin', tootin', shootin' Mexican bandit Pancho Villa. Seems it was President Wilson himself who dispatched troops to grab this South-of-the-Border nogoodnik, but Pancho proved to be ungrabbable, thus making Operation Pancho Villa one of President Woodrow Wilson's lousier fiascos.

70

Enjoying a roast not a Roast.

After the New Amsterdam Theatre opening in New York on a Sunday night, the Friars Frolic pushed to Philadelphia for a Monday matinee and then immediately segued on to Baltimore for a special command performance for Mr. Wilson. Backstage there was wall-to-wall nervousness about how the president would receive the humor in a theatre filled with Washington's elite. When the curtain rang down he sent a secret service agent to inform George M. Cohan he would like to meet the cast.

President Wilson solemnly shook hands with each member and when he neared George Sidney, the actor who played the part of Villa, the president said, "We've been looking for you all over Mexico and I find you here in Baltimore at a Friars Frolic!"

Abbot Cohan introduced a resolution right there to make the president an honorary Friar. The president approved. The officers and governors quickly seconded the motion and the president eagerly accepted. Thus, on the stage of the Old Ford Theatre in Baltimore in the year 1916 a president of the United States of America became a member of the Friars Club.

With such memory and such history in its background, the club has never tampered with tradition or the constitution that was created to make this a show-business club. There is an unwritten law that the abbot must be a show-business star. For this unpaid honor the club demands only the biggest. Well, since George M. we have done pretty good. You can't hardly get no bigger than the last four abbots—Milton Berle, Joe E. Lewis, Ed Sullivan, and a little blue-eyed singer you might have heard of called Frank Sinatra.

Another unwritten law is that the dean must be a former performer—actor, comic, hoofer, or burlesque banana, but he must be an entertainer turned businessman. Even though the executive director runs the club—and we have had two great ones in Carl Timin and now Walter Goldstein—it's the dean who is the VP and sort of chairman of the board of governors who balances the budget and keeps the peace as well as the club in the black.

The present dean, Buddy Howe, runs a pretty fair business of his own. He went from hoofer with Sammy Lewis and Patti Moore in 1925 to a flash act that played the Palace Theatre to an act billed as Howe, Leonard and Alyce which included Jack E. Leonard and Alyce Corell, wife of Charles Corell of Amos and Andy fame. After that it was Carroll and Howe until he joined the biggest show of all, the U.S. army, in 1942. While Buddy was dragging down his twelve bucks a month, his partner and wife, Jean Carroll, was earning $7,500 a week as a comedienne. Buddy made it back into show business as president of G.A.C., one of the major talent agencies, then chairman of the board of C.M.A., a giant talent agency, and now head of the personal appearance department of I.C.M. and vice-chairman of the board. When he merged General Artists Corporation and Creative Management Association to become International Creative Management, the largest theatrical agency in the world with a gross the first year of $250 million, Buddy accepted the call and became dean of the Friars.

It's practically a full-time job. There are over a thousand members and it's big business and the dean has to give it a lot of time and love. For this privilege he pays his dues like everybody else and pays his tabs more than everybody else. Besides that, he may be settling a big multimillion dollar business deal that includes Raquel Welch or Tom Jones or Engelbert Humperdinck or any one of his numberless star clients and some actor will holler over, "Hey, Dean, the eggs are cold."

The job of the dean is a little different now than it was when that handful Scotch-taped the club together seventy-three years ago.

The late Dean Harry Delf wrote this story in the Friars Frolic of 1949 that tells it like it was:

GREETINGS!

For the benefit of you who do not know, the Dean of the Friars is the Vice-President of the Club, but hardly the Throttlebottom that vice-presidents are generally considered to be. In the Friars, the Dean is a sort of Executive-Porter whose duties range anywhere between cajoling the members into paying their dues and flirting with the scrubwoman in order to get her best efforts in the Boys' Rooms. And somewhere mingled in between these and the more evident duties is the less romantic but more dangerous duty of keeping bridge players from killing each other; placating members' wives who insist over the phone that "He *is* there"; unraveling such mysteries as who took the Cavanaugh hat and left the Adams; finding the culprit that called Chicago last month on the Club telephone; assuring a member that his partner in the gin game didn't really mean it when he called him a moronic sonofasoandso 'cause he didn't knock with four; stopping those guys from goose-ing Charlie Hart, and reminding the kibitzers that they should stand and let the players sit. To these accomplishments has the Dean relegated his life.

Money was always the name of the game at the Friars—that is, the lack of it. Somehow they always had the shorts.

When they moved into the new club on 55th Street money was still scarce. Executive Director Carl Timin and the then manager, Walter Goldstein, went to all the "going out of business" auctions of restaurants to collect kitchen and bar equipment prompting press agent Friar Jack Cannon to remark, "Our clubhouse has been done in early Chapter 11."

When Dean Harry Delf died in 1964 abbot Joe E. Lewis cornered Buddy Howe and insisted that he take the job of dean and "just run the Club so we don't get in trouble. We actors need to have a place to hang around. We need somebody to take care of the business end. If you leave it to actors, we'll wind up living in the park. That's why we need agents or business managers—and you're both."

"I don't know if I can," Buddy said, "I have a list of actors I have to take care of now."

"Bring 'em in the club and take care of them here," he insisted. "Remember in 1932 when the Friars had the greatest actors in the world and they went bankrupt? Well, we need you to see that it doesn't happen again."

Dean Howe kept his word to Joe E. He brought Tom Jones and Engelbert Humperdinck and others on his client list into the club. He sold the Friars roasts to television and refused to accept a commission and thereby enriched the club's treasury by $200,000.

It still doesn't mean that one out-of-work juggler who's behind in his dues isn't going to attack him because his soup was cold or he didn't like his table at the Sinatra dinner.

I was on the fifth floor recently and looked through the window of the sauna and saw Buddy and confrere Abe Lastvogel in a heated discussion. I figured these two theatrical giants had to be discussing a multimillion dollar deal. When they came out I commented, "That must have really been a big deal in there—how much?" Buddy answered, "It wasn't a deal. Abe was just bawling me out because the cardroom needs painting."

When Buddy Howe and Jean Carroll were partners on stage as well as off, he saw her twenty-four hours a day. In the last years with the extra job as dean and the operation of I.C.M. and keeping his stars warm, although it's not exactly a hardship keeping Raquel Welch and Shirley MacLaine warm, Jean has been heard to heat up herself.

At the Dinah Shore dinner she really let him have it: "My husband was made president of television of G.A.C. and, of course, it affected our lives. There are a lot of pressures. It made him very nervous. He became a nail biter. Now this doesn't sound like much, but it's my nails that he's biting.

"He is so brainwashed . . . He only thinks in terms of TV. One night he came home and, it was novelty night, and I said, 'Honey, you know, it's been a long time, tonight it's Thursday night, things are quiet and it's 9:30, let's you and I retire early and have a little romance.' 'Are you kidding,' he hollered, 'you're opposite "The Untouchables." ' I think he has become one himself. I have to tell you a story about Buddy. Every time I did a shot on the Ed Sullivan show, I'd come home and my husband would be sitting there and he'd say, 'I know this guy has stayed up there for a long time, but why does he only give you four minutes? Why doesn't he know a comic like you needs a lot of time? Why does he always start out by opening the show with you?' I said, 'I don't know, all I know is that he pays pretty good.' So a number of months ago, my husband was made the head of the committee for the Cerebral Palsy telethon and he said, 'You going to come on the show, Jean?' and I said, 'sure you know I'll be happy to do anything I can.' So I walked in dressed up, in my fancy dress, and he gave me a very nice and impersonal nod and I said, 'Where am I on the show, honey?' and he said, 'you open.' 'How long do you want me to do?' and he said, 'do four minutes.' And I said, 'Okay, when you get home tonight, *you* get four minutes.' And you know something—he came home nineteen hours later and he didn't want the four minutes."

Buddy turned the entertainment chairmanship over to disc jockey William B. Williams. "I've seen a lot of stars born here since 1964," William B. told me, "and I saw one star die here . . . right in my arms."

September 7, 1966, was one of those unforgettable nights at the club, a black-tie salute to Joe E. with the jokes and the booze flowing to midnight. Sinatra, Buddy Hackett, Soupy Sales, Henny Youngman, Benny Davis, Nipsey Russell, Blossom Seeley, and Pat Henry all topped each other. William B. and comedian Alan Gale were the MC's.

Al Kelly, the beloved little double-talker, was the hit of the night. As the laughter soared he sat down. There was a standing ovation. He stood up to take another bow. Seconds later he collapsed. William B. took him in his arms but in the twinkling of an eye that it took Bill to cradle him, he was gone.

Blossom Seeley went on after Al Kelly without knowing anything happened. Blossom hobbled to the mike to sing "It Had to Be You" to the guest of honor.

"How old is she?" somebody asked. "I don't know," somebody else answered, "but she was singing at the time of the San Francisco earthquake in 1906." Even her husband, minstrel Benny Fields, supposedly hadn't known her age. This particular evening she seemed a little soft as she followed Kelly. Some people thought that she was just nervous after the big ovation that Al received. "I'm a little weak," she announced. A few bars into her song she began trembling and became faint.

"Get her off, she may be having a stroke!" somebody shouted.

The handsome silver-haired William B., who could attribute some of his gray hairs to this evening, thought it was a doubleheader for a moment. There were simultaneous commotions in the room. One group carried Al out. They laid him in the little bar, the Round the

75

World Room. Two physicians, Drs. Milton Reder and Saul Meylackson, members of the club, rushed after them and bent over Kelly.

There was no pulse. "He's through," one of them said. He had died three months before his seventieth birthday in his favorite club among his best friends, entertaining them up to the last minute of his life.

"If you have to go," Joe E. opined, "that's the way to do it, leave with the cheers ringing in your ears." Meanwhile, Blossom Seeley was gently taken from the platform by Jesse Block and delivered to her little room at the Park Central Hotel. After so many years of stardom Blossom was completely broke.

"I don't understand it," I said to Jesse, "Benny Fields and Blossom Seeley were headliners for years. Paramount did their life story, they made albums—where's the loot—what happened to it?"

"Room service," Jesse said. "They spent it all on room service. I don't think Bloss ever boiled water. If you came to my house, the Coke cost us a nickel and the booze came out of a bottle and Eve could always heat up a frank. But when you went to visit Bloss and Benny at the Warwick during all those years they lived there, everything was ordered from room service. Coke was a buck, each drink a couple of dollars, and every meal was a banquet ordered from room service. They had to go broke. Howard Hughes couldn't live like that. It's from all those years on the road and living on the run."

"Well," I asked, "what happened when Benny was gone and the money wasn't there?"

"Jack Benny, George Burns, and I saw to it that she still lived in the same style. See, when it was all gone, I talked to Jack and George about doing Friars luncheons in their honor with all the proceeds going to Blossom. Of course, they agreed and the Friars were able to keep Bloss in the style to which none of us ever became accustomed."

The Friars, with their acid-tongued roasts, would rather be known for insulting those they love than for the softhearted slobs they really are. "Softheaded is a better adjective," says Friar Groucho Marx.

In addition to raising over 25 million for charity, they do a loving job of caring for their own. Young new performers pay very little or nothing for the first couple of years until they get started. When infirm members can no longer work or take care of themselves, they're placed in actors' homes or nursing homes with the club footing the bills. Older members who can't afford the yearly dues are tactfully elected to a "senior membership."

A nonworking member who might be down on his luck can still enjoy the club at lunch or dinner and sign his tab including the tip and be treated like the star that he was. Very quietly his bill is submitted to and paid by the Joe E. Lewis fund for indigent actors, which also subsidizes his rent and wardrobe if and when help is needed. All such charitable deeds are strictly secret. The names of the recipients are guarded much more closely than the FBI files.

A Friar will always reach for a laugh to brush away the tear. He'll insist on turning everything into a joke. Charles Adler of the famous "Yacht Club Boys" nightclub act was always a smiling optimist even in the years before the quartet reached the big money. Adler was at the Monastery Round Table on the day the front pages reported Hitler's armies in sweeping triumph across Yugoslavia. Albeit the Friars were saddened by the war news, Adler reached for the newspaper and opened it to another page. "Look at you guys—just like actors, always seeing the darker side," he chided them. "There's a brighter side too: Rolls-Royce just dropped the price of its cars to $28,000."

Two of the famous fourteen karachters of the club were Barney Dean, the "ward" of Bob Hope and Bing Crosby, and Swifty Morgan who was the lifetime guest of Joe E. Lewis and Frank Sinatra.

Barney came from Hollywood for the testimonial to Bob Hope in New York as Bob's guest, of course. When he returned to California, his mother phoned to ask why he hadn't been home. "The Friars gave me a dinner," he said.

Sniffed his mother, "You come home and *I'll* give you a dinner. Better *they* should give you an overcoat."

When Swifty Morgan left New York to find his fame and fortune and a new touch or two in California, Joe E. gave him a letter to Sinatra. "Maybe he can do you some good," he said. "Only if he can cash a bad check," Swifty answered.

There is much good warm humor in our clubhouse. Take, for example, George Burns who is an actor-lover. I was kibitzing him at bridge in the cardroom. He was playing an unusually quiet game. "How come, George," I asked, "when you play bridge at the Friars in California you're always bawling someone out?" George quietly replied, "That's because these guys are better than me." I said, "So are the guys in California." He said, "Yes—but in California they're not actors!"

It was in the Friars poolroom that Jackie Gleason tried to pick a fight with little Alex Rose, the screenwriter who sees eye to eye with Mickey Rooney and Mayor Beame. "I'm half your size and weight, you big fat slob," Rose squealed, "why don't you pick on someone your own size?" Jackie answered, "Because I only hit women and midgets."

Songwriter George Meyer once became incensed at Mike, the Friars barber, because he went on vacation and wasn't around to shave him for a week. When Mike returned, Meyer threatened to have him fired. "Gee, Mr. Meyer," the barber pleaded, "you wouldn't do that. You wouldn't put me out of show business, would you?"

The Friars are not all fun and card games, however. There are more deals made in our clubrooms than at the U.N. There is more dealing going on in the steam room than in the cardroom.

Not long back William B. Williams, the prior, and Sammy Davis, Jr., the bard, met in the Joe E. Lewis room by planned accident and set themselves a TV deal that made them the Hansel and Gretel of the airwaves. I've seen I.C.M.'s Jackie Green sitting with Alan King in the dining room under the portrait of Will Rogers nailing a multimillion dollar deal for Barbra Streisand. Over a baby lobster at a Friday night shore dinner Jackie and booker Phil Greenwald agreed to put Raquel Welch into the Concord and by the time Jackie had sloshed his second claw through the melted butter they made the price.

Martin Bregman tied up Al Pacino and *Serpico* in the dining room and Howard Minsky tied down *Love Story* in the Milton Berle room. A scene in *The Sunshine Boys* was shot at the Friars. Don King, the greatest sports promoter of our time, discusses his next Muhammad Ali deals over his cocktail parties in the Joe E. Lewis room. Milton Rackmil of Universal and agents Lew Wasserman and Abe Lastvogel and Nat Lefkowitz have bought, sold, and exchanged galaxies of stars while stuffing themselves with bagels and lox at the Saturday buffet lunches.

Jackie Green, vice-president of I.C.M. and the admissions chairman of the Friars, signed a 2½-million-dollar contract for Shirley MacLaine sitting under a portrait of George M. Cohan at the Monastery. This picture was taken in Paris where Shirley explained America. She said that she was the only girl friend of J.F.K. that he talked to—"What's all the commotion about President Kennedy's love affairs? I'd rather he bleeped the girls than bleeped the country."

The old pros say that this was all amateur night compared to Mike Todd on the hustle. Old Todd-watchers insist Mike was the number one promoter of the century. Whenever you heard his name over the loudspeaker, "Friar Mike Todd—telephone please," you knew he was getting set to hustle some pigeon into something somewhere somehow.

The telephone bit is an archaic gimmick used to drum up instant popularity especially during election time when a guy's running for office, or when he needs to impress a client, or when he wants a little billing. Todd used it masterfully.

It was Mike's theory that you could not promote a sucker if you had to go to his office. Either he came to your turf or you met on neutral territory. "Okay, let's meet for lunch where we can have a nice quiet talk." Todd invariably grabbed the first table in the Friars' dining room where everybody knew him and he was bound to be interrupted.

He welcomed interruptions because they gave him time to formulate answers and to impress his potential backers with celebrities. He figured if the angel shook hands with Milton Berle or Bob Hope he had already gotten his money's worth. He figured the prospect (or suspect) was already ahead because it gave him an opening gambit with his wife that night.

Todd also arranged to have his office telephone him at intervals. The paging was music to his ears. The conversations (all imaginary) were shrewdly calculated to buff up his reputation to the unsuspecting investors at the table by presenting him as a producer of taste and integrity:

> "L.B., you'll blow the studio if you go ahead with that script. They'll murder you."
>
> "Gee, Mr. Lee, you need money. I'll have my man bring you over some."
>
> "I don't need that kind of money. You'll want me to put your mother-in-law in the chorus and I'll blow a million dollars for your lousy ten G's."
>
> "Jack, I told you before I don't need money that badly."

Mike had his way of making a "full disclosure." He said, "I don't want any partners in my production. It's a Mike Todd Production. And I want all the credit. And if I'm wrong, the critics will bat my brains in, not yours. I know my racket and I don't want you to think that I am robbing you. I want to spend the money my way. I once threw a scene out because it didn't smell right to my kisser. If I have to come to mugs like you, you'll make me nervous.

"I'll make it simple. I am not a businessman—that's why we're going to make a lot of money together. You loan me fifty big ones. And I'll put you down on the books and every week you come around the theatre and get yourself two G's. In one year you'll make yourself 145 percent on your dough without any risk. This is a safe, nice conservative investment. And, if you're not greedy, you'll jump for it. You're too smart a guy for me to fool you with phony statements and besides I don't have the time to steal money that way.

"Waiter, give me the check."

The setting of the Friars helped pretty good too. The members have been capitalizing on the setting for years. If the Friars charged

5 percent for every deal set at the club, nobody would ever have to pay dues and they could run the Monastery forever.

The Friars Club is a membership of talent and not all of the greatest showmen are in front of the curtain, either. Damon Runyon used to tell the story of how he got his first newspaper job. It happened in Denver. He sat in the outer office patiently waiting while an office boy carried in his request to be seen by the busy editor.

In about ten minutes the boy came back and said, "He wants you to send in a card." Runyon had no card, but being resourceful he reached into his pocket and pulled out a deck of cards. He carefully extracted an ace and said, "Give him this!" He got in and got the job.

Of course, there's many a deal that unfolds at the club where a nickel never changes hands. Every civilian who enrolls in the Monastery looks to mingle with the pros. After he buys you the first Diet Pepsi he gives you the opportunity to entertain at his son's Bar Mitzvah, "Be my guest—all the food and drinks on the house —and if you feel like getting up and saying a few cracks—it's okay by me—you don't have to do more than twenty minutes."

Comedy writer Eli Basse is always an easy touch for a square who needs an opener for a speech he's making at a Kiwanis meeting or a zinger of a line for his office party. The only thing that bothers Eli is when the schnook asks him to rewrite the gag because, "My wife says it's too fresh—ain't you got something funny but nice?—and put in something serious."

Goodman Ace is a distinguished comedy writer. He is distinguished by the fact that his take-home pay for writing the Perry Como Show was in the neighborhood of $10,000 a week. Goody also knocked off five figure type salaries for scribbling comedy gems for such shows as Tallulah Bankhead and Milton Berle. Goody wouldn't even burp for under five thou.

Enter into the club one fine afternoon a doctor Friar. The doctor Friar has a wife. The wife is having a birthday. The doctor spies Goody. Over he lumbers and says, "As one Friar to another, how about writing something funny for my wife's birthday cake?"

I don't know what Goody's terse answer to the doctor was but the fellows sitting around told me that the one line was worth fifteen hundred.

One Saturday lunch I got in trouble with a big-shot judge who pestered me to put together a routine for him. He was to speak at an important Republican convention and ". . . only you can write the crap they'll like." I stayed up all night trying to give him the material that "only I can write." I even rehearsed him in the part. He saw me a few days later at the club and hollered, "Your speech laid an egg, do me a favor, give your jokes to the Democrats from now on." Not only didn't he pay me and not only did he insult me but I got stuck with his tab for lunch!

I don't want you to gather from these stories that the pros are strictly on a cash and carry-on basis. Oscar-winning songwriters Jule Styne and Sammy Cahn have given up paid assignments to work for free on a Friars Frolic.

Oscar Hammerstein labored as hard on a Frolic as for any of his own shows and for much less royalties and so did ASCAP greats Stanley Adams, Mitchell Parish, Lou Alter, Benny Davis, Irving Caesar, and Ned Washington.

Writers George S. Kaufman, Jack Lait, Sime Silverman, stars Walter Kelly, James J. Corbett, and so many others have contributed their stories and talent to the Friars *Epistles* and Friars *Fables* —and I do mean contributed. All strictly on the arm.

"It's been that way from the time Victor Herbert and Charles Emerson Cook scratched out "The Friars Song" and Enrico Caruso sang it right up to the most recent dinner where Sammy Cahn and Jule Styne collaborated on a song for Robert Merrill to sing to old Blue Eyes—all for charity.

The Bobby Gordons and Buddy Arnolds who wrote many of the Frolics as well as the roasts not only contributed their talents but paid their own dues and their tabs as well. In some cases the stars who appeared on the dais also paid their way and they are and were the biggest in the business.

Take the Frolic of 1939. Jay C. Flippen was committee chairman and the stars that appeared that April 9 at the Alvin Theatre were:

Milton Berle	Abbott and Costello	Harry Richman
Georgie Jessel	Benny Fields	Buster Shaver
Olsen and Johnson	Bert Frohman	Eddie Miller and Choir
Lou Holtz	Eddie Garr	Sophie Tucker
Ben Bernie	Jimmy Durante	Helen Morgan
Lew Lehr	Henny Youngman	Josephine Huston
Harry Hershfield	Walter (Dare) Wahl	Hildegarde
Bill Robinson	Joe E. Lewis	Wini Shaw
Smith and Dale	Jerry Kruger	The Hot Mikado Co.

Show people offer their talents and their hearts easily. Just don't use them wrongly. One manufacturer approached Sammy Cahn to write a special lyric for his office party: "You can use your song 'Three Coins in a Fountain' but just change the words around to fit my organization—you know, say something funny—"

Sammy said, "Tell me, mister, what business are you in?"

"I manufacture ladies' handbags, the most expensive in the country, they sell them at all the leading department stores and. . . ."

"I tell you what I'm gonna do, send me a dozen handbags so I can give them to all my friends, and I'll write your song."

"Hey," the guy said, "I'm a fellow Friar, what do you mean, send you a dozen handbags? Those things cost a lot of money."

"So do my songs," said Sammy as he walked away.

Show people are only beautiful. When an actor tells you, "I've got good news for you" the good news he's got for you is something about himself. There was the night Sophie Tucker invited Burns and Allen, Block and Sully, Jack Benny and Mary Livingstone, and some other pages of *Who's Who* to her home to give them some good news. The good news was that she just made a big album of her songs. The bad news was that she then sold them to her guests for ten bucks apiece. The other good news was that the money went to charity.

You can't top actors. Recently another eighty-six shares of stock were transferred from Adah Lewis, Ted Lewis's wife, into the Joe E. Lewis Fund. That's why this nonprofit organization rewards so many with honorary memberships because they worked for others. Joe Smith of Smith and Dale is an honorary member after paying dues and working for free for a hundred years. So are Jack Dempsey, John Lindsay, Hubert Humphrey, Bing Crosby, and Mayor Beame.

Again, I say show people are only beautiful—they're easy marks for any charity even if it's for the prevention of athlete's foot as long as it offers some kind of award: Man of the Year, Boy of the Week, Jew of the Block, anything they can hang on the wall at home.

Jerry Lewis knows the award is a gimmick to get free entertainment but he can't refuse a good cause. Jerry was actually elated when a national organization approached him at the Friars and said, "Not only because you're a fellow-Friar, but we have taken a poll of our members from coast to coast and we decided unanimously to make you the Man of the Year—you are the only one we want."

"Thanks," Jerry said proudly as he brushed away a tear, "when is the affair?" "August fifteenth," the chairman beamed. "August fifteenth!" Jerry said sadly. "Gee, I'm sorry. I'll be in Europe making a picture then." "Too bad," said the chairman, "can you suggest anybody else?"

Howard Cosell was sitting at a corner table with Milton Berle one lunchtime when Jean-Pierre walked over and said, "Mr. Cosell, it's an unwritten law at the club that you can't bother celebrities, but now that you're a member I hope you don't mind signing some autographs, I told them I would ask you first, I hope you don't mind the interruption."

Cosell said, "Well, Milton and I are trying to work out a show here, but I guess it's okay. But look, not more than a dozen, you understand, we're busy. No more than twelve."

"But Mr. Cosell," Jean-Pierre said, "there are only two."

How are you going to explain show people? Eli Basse wished me a "Happy New Year" and then added, "and this year I mean it."

8

Abbot
Joe E. Lewis
1953-1971

When Joe E. Lewis was elected abbot in 1953 the Friars were awarded an honorary liquor license. Joe E., one of the last of the red-hot boozers, boasted of the fact that in his honor they redecorated the bar. Quoth Joe: "They put new drunks around it."

A pixie with longtime scars hemstitched in his face from the time the Chicago boys decided to give him a little unasked-for plastic surgery, Joe always claimed he was not a big drinker: "I just put away a lot of little ones." He insisted that he knew his capacity for liquor: "The only trouble is I get drunk before I reach it."

In an era when saloons constituted the big-time entertainment, when nightclubs weren't just Las Vegas and naked chorus broads and bus tours with two drinks apiece, when there were a half-dozen gin mills in every city like, for instance, the Roosevelt in New Orleans; the Mocambo and Ciro's in Hollywood; the Beachcomber, the Latin Quarter, and the Five O'Clock Club in Miami; the Latin Quarter, Leon and Eddie's, the Riviera, the China Doll, the Hollywood, the Paradise, and Copacabana in New York—in those days Joe E. was the king.

In an age when the maître d' with the small smile and the large palm was divinity, when you tipped a C-note for a ringside table, when the measure of your status was if you could shoulder your way into the Copa past the civilians behind the silken rope at 12:20 in the morning and nail a table for four on the ring for the 12:30 show—in those days Joe E. was the king.

He was a comic-storyteller-singer who would jazz up his double-entendre lyrics with a little two-step. He danced like a demented penguin, croaked like a frog with laryngitis, did jokes so blue even Johnny Carson would have blushed, and punctuated each with another pull from the Scotch glass that was permanently implanted in his right hand. With Joe E. to be shicker was to be normal and it was the hell with the doctors, the warnings about liquor, the diabetes, the daily injections, and the half a stomach. He was going to live it up while he was here.

Joe E.'s reign as abbot lasted from 1953 to 1971, which will always be gift wrapped as the swinging years at the Friars . . . especially when he was in residence. He held court every night in the Joe E. Lewis Room which is one flight up in the Friars clubhouse at 57 East 55th Street. It's a man's room but much prettier now that women are admitted at night. It's paneled in wood from the British Honduras with stained-glass windows and a stone fireplace.

The paintings on the wall are of the present and past abbots including George M. Cohan, Bob Hope, Milton Berle, Frank Sinatra and, of course, Joe E. Lewis. Any Friar would rather have his portrait hanging there than in the Metropolitan Museum.

"You only live once," the abbot liked to say while hoisting his glass, "but if you live it right—once is enough." Or "May the Good Lord take a liking to you—but not too soon."

Joe E.'s semisparse brown hairs were parted neatly and, like any other well-heeled Jewish boy of the period, he sported the proverbial diamond ring on his right hand but outside of that he didn't do anything the way anybody else did. A pal of gents, touts, jockeys, millionaires, hoofers, and hookers, Joe never went to bed late. Never ever later than noon. And he was an early riser. Never laid around in bed later than five in the afternoon. And he always ate a good-sized dinner about an hour after he got up—in case he should forget about food later. And he always lived in a hotel, the Warwick in New York.

A Tab Hunter he wasn't. An average-sized man with an average-sized paunch and a ready smile he was. But he always had women. The truth is, Joe E. wasn't a ladies' man. He was a man's man. He preferred the four-legged ponies to the two-legged ones and a crap table to a kitchen table.

Another Friar, Will Rogers, once said, "I never met a man I

An X-rated party for Joe E. Left to right, Gary Morton, Gene Baylos, Berle, Henny, the Ritz Brothers, Olsen and Johnson, Johnny Puleo, Jerry Lewis, Jan Murray, Joe E. Lewis, and assorted comics of various shapes, sizes, billings, and bankrolls.

didn't like." Joe E. said that every girl he went with felt the same way. Conversely, I never met a man, woman, or tout who didn't like Joe E. And he loved the world: "There's a little good in everything—even a Mickey Finn has a couple of drops of bonded whiskey in it." Joe E. loved everybody "except a camel, or anybody else who doesn't take a drink once in a while."

Lewis, of course, was the easiest touch at the Friars. He was a sucker for a guy with his hand out. One casual racetrack acquaintance petitioned him for "twenty bucks—I got a sure thing in the next at Pimlico." Joe handed him the money and that night received his twenty back. The next day the same character made another request—this time for fifty dollars. After the last race he refunded the loan. On the third day when he asked for a hundred, Joe waved him away, "Nothing doing!" rasped Joe. "You fooled me twice!"

Joe E. once gave a panhandler a dollar for a drink and followed him up the street until the bum got nervous. "I just wanted to make sure," our boy told him, "that you didn't waste the money on a bowl of soup."

Our abbot became ill from "living it right" and his Friar pals knew he was in trouble when he said, "If I had to live my life over again I wouldn't have the strength."

His buddy, Frank Sinatra, who played Joe E. Lewis on the screen, really loved Joe. He flew cross-country just to have a talk with him. "You know I love you, Everglades," Frank said softly, using his pet nickname, "but you've got to take it easy. I'm known to take a drink or two myself but you're ridiculous. If you're going to drink like a fish, you should drink what a fish drinks."

"I know I promised I'd stop drinking," Joe E. whispered, "but I didn't promise I'd stop lying."

The abbot emeritus, Milton Berle, tried to help. "They say drinking shortens a man's life." "Yes," Joe smiled, "but he sees twice as much in the same length of time."

Everybody tried but none succeeded. "I only drink to get rid of warts and pimples," he explained to his drinking pal Jackie Gleason, "not from me but from people I talk to."

Ed Sullivan really worked on him. "You're going to be the toastmaster at my Friars roast," he pleaded. "I want you to stay sober. You've got to try," Ed said seriously, "you only have one life. I know—I know your answer, if you live it right, once is enough. But this isn't living right. You've got to make a real effort to get into shape."

Slowly Joe came back with, "People say I'm never sober. That's a lie. Why I've been sober four times today."

"The jokes are funny," Ed said somberly, "but your situation is not. Your friends are worried about you. Please do what we ask and stop drinking for a while." The trouble is Joe E. was committed to booze and gambling as a way of life. He continued to have twenty or thirty Scotches a night despite his doctor's warnings, reinforcing his habit with "I know more old drunks than old doctors."

You know something? We believed him. We figured his connection was better than ours. That is, until that day when he was taken to the hospital. Dean Buddy Howe called a special meeting of the board of governors to pray for our beloved abbot. There wasn't a dry throat or a dry eye as we sat around telling Joe E. stories in the room named after him.

Proctor Jack Benny told about the time our boy met Harry Truman at the White House. The president asked if there was anything he could do for him. "Well," said Joe E., "I've had some bad horses lately, Mr. President, can you get me an advance on my Social Security?"

Prior Phil Silvers regaled us of when Joe E. was decorating the bar at the Copa. A man who was escorting three girls told Joe: "I'm cutting down on my smoking. May I borrow a cigarette?" "Sure," cracked Joe E., handing him one. "By the way, I'm cutting down on girls, may I borrow one of yours?"

Red Buttons, the secretary of the Friars, related the familiar story of the obsequious fan who kept interrupting Joe E.'s drinking. For the first ten minutes he was only a pest, but after that he became annoying. Finally the guy burbled, "I think you're the greatest—what else can I say?" "You can say 'good-bye,'" Joe E. suggested.

Earl Wilson told us about the time he was describing the 1929 crash where billions were lost and so many were ruined and Joe E. interjected: "An average day in Las Vegas."

"Joe E. used to say," Monk Robert Merrill reminded us, "Las Vegas is the only town in the country where you can have a good time without enjoying yourself."

"I'll never forget," Ed Sullivan spoke up, "the time he introduced

Mitzie Green and Joe E.

Friar Georgie Jessel as a man who just reached middle age for the third time."

Alan King, the monitor of the Friars, told about the night in honor of Gene Baylos. Gene did a good bit of Joe E.'s routine that night, and right before, Joe was introduced to say something nice about Baylos. "I like Gene," he said, "he's got very witty ears."

Bing Crosby, George Burns, Alan King, Joey Bishop, Don Rickles,

Johnny Carson, Sammy Davis, Jr., Myron Cohen, William B. Williams each came up with a Joe E. Lewis line:

"The recession doesn't bother me. I went broke during the boom."

"I saw that picture where two couples jump into bed together—that's making four the hard way."

"Anybody takes me for a fool makes no mistake."

"I follow the horses. Trouble is, the horses I follow follow the horses."

"I've been rich and I've been poor. Believe me, rich is better."

"You think I drink? They gave Dean Martin a hotfoot—he burned for three days."

"Phil Harris sees a psychiatrist once a week to make him stop drinking—and it works. Every Wednesday between five and six he doesn't touch a drop."

"I know a lady eighty-five doesn't need glasses—drinks right out of the bottle."

His beloved pal and writer Eli Basse reminded us that Joe's wife of two years, the beautiful blonde actress-singer Martha Stuart, wanted to sue the Friars for alienation of affections. Joe loved Martha but "she doesn't like staying up with the fellas and how would it look if I didn't close up the bar?"

The meeting adjourned when we decided to go see Abbot Lewis and bring him a little love. Milton Berle, the abbot emeritus, was chosen to head the delegation. We were all ready to shoot from the lip but as usual our beloved Joe beat us to the punch lines: "They told me I was in ill health," he started, "I found out I have no health at all." Joe didn't give us a chance to cheer him. He was too fast for us: "I was feeling lousy, then I took a sudden turn for the nurse." You couldn't stop him: "My operation lasted five hours. It was wonderful—first good night's sleep I had in three years. I'm responsible for a new surgical technique—instead of stitches they used cork."

What we didn't know is that right after the operation he insisted that the doctor sneak his writer Eli Basse up to his room to get him ready for us. Joe hated sympathy. All he wanted was to make others happy. "They cut me," he greeted us, "first time the doctor ever saw blood with a head on it. The doctor says I'll have to live on nothing but food and water for at least a week. I told the doctor I only drink to quiet my nerves. He said nobody's nerves are that noisy. Do you know my doctor gives plaid stamps? Two more operations and I get a pair of roller skates."

We were all masters of the spoken word. All of us gathered in that room made our living by speaking. And yet the most dramatic dialogue of all was unfolding silently. None of us were saying what we all knew—that this was Joe E.'s last routine.

Berle could only offer a toast—the same one that Joe E. had used a thousand times at post time: "You only live once. But if you do it right, once is enough."

The next day when Jacqueline Susann came by to hold his hand, he said to her in a barely audible whisper, "You know something, Honey, I was wrong—once is not enough."

It's the first time Joe E. Lewis made us cry.

9

The Friars
of California

Georgie Jessel was reminiscing. Georgie Jessel is always reminiscing. He was reminiscing when he was six years old about the time he had his first girl—and he's been lying about those things ever since.

When you get to be Jessel's age you automatically earn reminiscing rights. The older a man gets the further back he remembers. He was nine years old when he and Walter Winchell and Eddie Cantor were a team and they lived next door to each other in East Harlem. As he tells it now they were three years old and he had his first affair with Betsy Ross or Florence Nightingale or somebody like that.

Jessel like to reminisce about the presidents whom he made laugh and he can go back to every one of them from Ford to his pal Harry Truman to Chester Arthur and John Quincy. And if he really gets on a sentimental kick about those halcyon days, he might wheeze on about how he spoke at the welcome dinner to Christopher Columbus with his pal Sitting Bull who was chairman of the affair.

As Georgie tells it: "In 1956 I had the privilege and the honor to be shaking the warm hand of the Dowager Queen of England, mother of this Elizabeth. She is the most beautiful mature woman I have ever met. Awful flirt that I am (or was), I couldn't resist saying to her, 'Ma'am, I doubt whether we shall ever meet again and I am sure, if so, not under these, for me, intimate circumstances. So I dare tell you, if you had no title at all and I saw you on the street, I would whistle and follow you up an alley.' I held my breath with visions of the palace guards throwing me bodily out of Victoria Palace. Then the Queen Mother answered, 'How charming of you, Mr. Jessel.'"

So far, Georgie has no tales about his romances with Joan of Arc or Helen of Troy for which I am very grateful.

His pal Eddie Cantor once told me: "With apologies to Budd Schulberg, here's my idea of 'What Makes Jessel Run.' Georgie has always had a head start for two reasons: lots of nerve and no nerves. Worry is just a word to him—nothing more. He's a fast man with a dollar and a doll—figures there's always more where they came from. Of course, his alimony has cost a small fortune (mine), but I can't complain, Georgie always paid me back. Even if he didn't, I couldn't kick. Many's the time, back in the early days, Jessel's way with women paid off for me, too. For example:

"We were playing together in Gus Edwards's *Kid Kabaret* and though Gus paid us very well we were almost always broke. Georgie took care of his mamma uptown in New York and I sent a weekly money order to my grandmother on the Lower East Side. We just had to find ways and means of eating for free. What schemes!

"One night in San Francisco, Georgie burst into the dressing room: 'Eddie, don't worry, I met a girl whose father owns a restaurant—she's crazy about me—brother are we going to eat!' And for two weeks did we eat! Breakfast, lunch, dinner, snacks! But you know something? You can get pretty sick of that chow mein."

When Georgie reads, he uses a monocle. "I'd rather be called eccentric than get a Seeing Eye dog," he says. "I'm too old to see without glasses." At the Friars one noon, monocle and all, our Harlem Disraeli was scanning the menu. "What's the matter, Georgie," inquired Fred Allen, "doesn't the other eye eat?"

Dubbed toastmaster-general of the United States, my pal Jessel has less schooling than anyone in show business, yet his knowledge of speech would make Bill Buckley sound like he was tongue-tied. Cantor said: "Georgie has entertained not only presidents but kings —Director Henry King, Nat King Cole, and King Kong."

Well, in between his reminiscing and his entertaining presidents, kings, and *kurvehs*, Jessel was forming the Friars Club of California. Jonie Taps, the then vice-president of Columbia Pictures, called a meeting in his office at the studio and invited Abbott and Costello, George Raft, Bing Crosby, and Georgie himself to discuss the idea. It was unanimous that Jessel become the first abbot.

When Harry Cohn, the president, czar, and dictator of Columbia, was clued in by his spies that Jonie was entertaining the biggest names in show business in his office, he summoned him to his throne

room and demanded to know what picture he was doing behind his back with these big names? When Jonie explained that he was organizing a West Coast Friars, Cohn said, "Okay. Put me down as a charter member. Do charter members have to pay dues?"

The first scene of the Friars Club of California was laid at the Savoy Hotel in Beverly Hills on January 15, 1947. A cast of over fifty theatrical giants showed up to listen to the first abbot lay out the plot, but not before a bit of reminiscing, of course:

"Too many years ago I became a member of the Friars Club of New York. The abbot was without question the most important member of the entertainment industry in the whole world, George M. Cohan. We had a star-spangled club, the character of whose membership has never been equaled by any theatrical organization in any country—until now. We featured such members as Woodrow Wilson, Enrico Caruso, Will Rogers, Jimmy Walker, Franklin Delano Roosevelt, and almost every man of prominence.

"In the theatrical upheaval that came about, many of the greats of show business migrated out here and Hollywood became the show-business capital of the world. Now it is suggested to me and Mr. Crosby, Mr. Hope and Bob Taylor that such a club and such a group might be arranged right here on the West Coast to carry on in the tradition of the old Friars Club."

Georgie suggested himself as abbot "with your approval, of course," Bing Crosby as dean, Robert Taylor as prior, Jimmy Durante as herald, and William Penzer as secretary-treasurer. They were all elected on the spot. They all accepted on the same spot.

To keep the history book straight, Jonie Taps became chairman of the board of governors with a team consisting of Irving Briskin, Pat O'Brien, Bud Abbott, Lou Costello, Al Lichtman, George Raft,

Abe Shore, Frank Morgan, Maurice Grudd, Harry James, Mickey Rooney, Irving Mills, Cecil B. DeMille, and Danny Winkler.

Jessel also appointed an entertainment committee that was a pretty good show package even if nobody else showed up, George Burns, Groucho Marx, Frank Sinatra, and Al Lichtman.

One member asked, "We know everybody here—all the officers and board of governors and all—but who is William Penzer? And why is he secretary-treasurer?" Jessel barked, "He is the owner of the building—$366,000 worth and he put up all the early money—any other silly questions?"

"We are ready to go," Georgie told his all-star audience. "The clubroom will be at 8428 Sunset and it will be great with a steam room, massage room, cardroom, sun deck, cardroom, handball courts, gym—outdoor and indoor—and a cardroom.

"There will be a billiards, pool, dining room, cardroom, library, cardroom, electrical cabinets, cards in the electric cabinets, and each cabinet equipped with a midget bookmaker.

"Like in the old days of the Friars in New York, no women will enter here. That's nothing to applaud about—it's a sorry thing. However, for the bachelor it will be a place to be phoned. For the married man on the night out it will do away with having to stay up with the sick lodge friend. Like the old judge used to say, 'It is a place where your home folks will know that this is where you are playing cards.' "

As it turned out the Friars of California is strictly a man's club. Women can come for Sunday brunch or Thursday buffet but the rest is strictly monk time. There is nothing doing at night. But that's true of all of Hollywood. No matter how beautiful and hot it gets during the day—there is still nothing to do at night—unless it's a card game—and the Friars of California would rather not talk about that at the moment—or any moment.

Jessel promised it would be a very private and intimate fraternity. "After all, it would be awfully difficult to have a club where a lot of fellows would be continually asking Harry Cohn or Jack Warner or Darryl Zanuck, 'What is that thing you're doing—and why haven't you used me in it?'

"This is a small town. Pick a fight with Zanuck or Warner and before it's over, Romanoff and Chasen know about it and they won't give you a table."

The club started with 130 members 95 percent of whom were in show business. Under the charter of the New York Friars as a subsidiary, it guaranteed reciprocal respect for each other's members plus the use of the facilities. The California Friars can sign in New York but the New York Friars must ante up cash in California. Being a New Yorker I will not make one single solitary comment about this arrangement even if California does pay a yearly stipend to New York for the use of the name.

Naturally Georgie Jessel was the first guest of honor at the first roast of the Friars West. It took place at the Biltmore Hotel in Los Angeles in 1948. Georgie's only regret was that he couldn't be his own toastmaster, so he appointed Jack Benny to do the chores. "Jessel did everything in his power to take this job away from me," Benny said, "he wanted to be the guest of honor and the toastmaster but fortunately, ladies and gentlemen, I happen to be an officer of the Friars and I put a stop to it.

"I am the proctor of the Friars. I was elected to that high post about three months ago. The proctor of the Friars is equivalent to a photographer on the *Reader's Digest*. That's why I am so proud to introduce Georgie Jessel who has the unique distinction of being the only American mentioned in *Who's Who* and the *Kinsey Report*."

Bob Hope said: "Georgie used to work as a producer for Darryl Zanuck at Twentieth Century. He was really the key man out there. Every time Zanuck went to the men's room Jessel handed him the key.

"Jessel is a loyal fellow. He was crazy about his boss. I can just see the scene that night at the Academy Awards. When Darryl bent over to kiss the Oscar, Jessel bent over to kiss Zanuck. I can't tell you what he does to keep his job, but he didn't get bad breath from kissing Zanuck's hand."

Al Jolson reminded us that "years ago Georgie Jessel was starring on Broadway in *The Jazz Singer* and he was a sensation. But when Jack Warner made the picture of *The Jazz Singer* he starred me in the role. Well, naturally this upset Jessel and Georgie took an oath that he'd break Jack Warner if it took his last cent. Warner doesn't know this, but he's only got about two weeks to go because Jessel's down to his last $120—if Georgie happens to meet a girl tonight, Warner will be broke tomorrow."

George Burns said, "Jessel's performance in *The Jazz Singer* just took me apart. I cried like a baby. When he finished 'Kol Nidre'

I ran backstage with tears streaking down my face to congratulate him. But Jessel's publicity man, Bennett, was standing outside his dressing room and wouldn't let me in. He said, 'You can't go in. Jessel has all his clothes off.' I said, 'What's that got to do with it? I've seen a naked Jew before. I want to tell him how great he was.' Bennett said, 'Not now—he's got a girl in there who he's putting into show business.' And I thought nothing could follow 'Kol Nidre!' "

Jack Carter: "Georgie is an unhappy man. He just got his first anti-Semitic letter and it was in Yiddish."

Georgie Jessel answered: "I am not a rich man but whatever I have is profit. I began with nothing—not only that—after I was a few days old they took something away from me."

When the comedians lumbered west to where the spotlight was brighter, so did the roasts and the roasters. The Friars Frolics were bigger than ever. In one show Clark Gable, Ronald Reagan, and Danny Kaye were in the chorus and Ben Blue, Donald O'Connor, and George Burns were in the ballet—all to raise money for the Motion Picture Actors' Home and to feed a thousand or more indigent actors and their families on Thanksgiving and Christmas and to take care of those performers who couldn't take care of themselves.

The Friars of California gave more dinners than the Salvation Army—only the prices were higher and the ham thicker. The roasts were especially well done. Somehow the high and mighty of the industry feel honored to be hacked to pieces by the D'Artagnans of the spoken word.

Even the unapproachable Sam Goldwyn appeared to like it when Groucho Marx ripped him at one Friars roast. After Groucho introduced him, Goldwyn made a less than thrilling speech about the glories of being an independent producer. When he sat down Groucho slunk to the microphone, flicked the ashes from his cigar, glared at Goldwyn, and sneered, "Do you suppose I could buy back that introduction?" Then he turned to the audience and growled, "I saw Mr. Goldwyn's latest picture and what he's got to be independent about, I'll never know."

When Leo Durocher accepted the honor of being mauled for charity, Jesse Block asked him publicly, "You'd rather be known as a nice guy than a good manager, right?" Leo said, "Right." "You're full of *bleep*," said Jesse.

Harry Cohn glowed when Johnny Carson laid it on him with, "Mr. Cohn has the personality of the back wall of a handball court." And Carson loved Phil Silvers's: "I'd like to introduce Bob Hope but I'm stuck with Johnny Carson. Johnny is the only Gentile on the dais and immediately after his speech we are going to circumcise him."

Milton Berle said at one dinner, "I don't want to stand here and tell a lot of old jokes but I'd like to introduce a guy who will—Henny Youngman." Henny rattled off a string of one-liners. When he sat down Berle burped, "Thank you for that soon-to-be-forgotten performance."

The Friars had so many big names left over they honored three of them at once in 1963: the costars of *Mad, Mad, Mad World*, Milton Berle, Phil Silvers, and Buddy Hackett. The event at the Beverly Hilton Hotel served two purposes. It permitted the Friars to fry the comedians who are active members and it increased the collections for the Charity Foundation to more than three million.

The gavel was handed to Jessel who used it as a meat cleaver in traditional style. "The poet Robert Burns in a melancholy mood once wrote: 'The best laid plans of mice and men gang aft aglee.' For the non-Scotch it means: The plans of all living things, no matter how great or small, do not end the way they are planned—our fall from grace is self-explanatory on this occasion tonight. This evening had been planned as a dinner for the president of the United States—and *look what we got*—Berle, Silvers, and Hackett."

"That's because Hart Schaffner and Marx didn't want it," Red Buttons added. "And Castro, Nasser, and Gene Baylos weren't available," Jessel cracked.

Eddie Cantor said, "For years the Friars have always roasted the ones they love—tonight we break that tradition in honoring Milton, Phil, and Buddy." Eddie talked about "one of the nicest guys in or out of show business, Phil Silvers. At one time, years ago, Phil had a crush on Olivia De Havilland. She went out with him several times, but when he asked her to the Academy Awards dinner, social high mark of the season, she said, 'I'll go with you on one condition—that you don't wear those silly glasses.' Phil promised to do without them and kept his word. He arrived at her door that evening in white tie and tails with a corsage of orchids and a Seeing Eye dog."

"When Buddy Hackett was born," Art Linkletter said, "he was

a six-pound mouth." Buddy answered lovingly, "Up your *bleep*—this whole dinner is a lot of bull*bleep* and you can all kiss my *bleep*."

Berle let all the comics answer for him. Jack Carter grunted: "Jessel is the world's youngest dirty old man. Look at those medals on his rented USO soldier suit. The only thing he ever attacked was Sophie Tucker in her dressing room at Loew's State."

Jan Murray: "Jessel has done so much for the glorious state of Israel. As you all know, one time it was just a desert—but he helped to plant trees, homes, hospitals, schools, and an airport—can you imagine what he could have done if he didn't have a hernia?"

"Look what this man has contributed to show business. Do you realize Georgie Jessel was the first comedian to do jazz songs on Broadway? He was the first comedian to use a telephone in a monologue, but most important he was the first comedian to be tried under the Mann Act. That was the time he carried Sophie Tucker over the state line. How do you think he got the hernia?"

Jessel returned the compliment to Berle: "Miltie, even as a babe suckling at a midwife's breast, stole her lavaliere."

At the dinner for Jack L. Warner, Frank Sinatra unleashed this: "Georgie's been working under a great handicap tonight because our guest of honor is still alive . . . The Warner Brothers showed the town the real meaning of brotherhood—they were brothers and they were hoods. As for Jack Warner's charity—the United Jewish Appeal don't have to call on him and beg every year. They just send over two Jewish gangsters to beat him up."

Bob Hope said at the Arnold Palmer roast: "I wear Arnold Palmer shirts, Arnold Palmer shoes, Arnold Palmer pants, but I play golf like Betsy Palmer."

Stan (The Man) Musial was roasted to a crisp char by Gene Autry: "He is not only a great ballplayer but a gentleman. He reminds me of Saint Paul—one of the dullest towns in America."

Hal Kemp, who has discovered and booked more talent than any man in the business, was discovered by the Friars at a dinner on his fiftieth year as a talent booker. Ed Wynn said: "Kemp has booked more stars than the Beverly Hills vice squad."

Red Buttons at the Sammy Davis, Jr., blast: "Sammy was brought up in a poor colored family—and grew up in a rich Jewish home."

Morey Amsterdam in honoring Bing Crosby: "With his great song, 'Love Thy Neighbor,' he did so much good. He started more wife swapping than any man in our history."

Bob Hope in dishonoring me: "Joey Adams received an honorary law degree at a Chinese university. I am told that a horse once graduated with an honorary degree from this institution. It was the first time in history a college gave an honorary degree to an *entire* horse."

The Friars West have roasted everybody from Don Rickles to Mae West and Harry Richman to Gary Cooper and Desi and Lucy. Always the butt of honor has a chance to hit back—except in the case of Desi Arnaz and Lucille Ball.

Mae West was still inviting the men in her audience to "come up and see me sometime" . . . even if she forgot what she wanted to see them about. Gary Cooper didn't have much to say after "yup" except that he was proud of the fact that he was the only one in Hollywood who had Buster Crabbe's unlisted phone number.

Don Rickles, as usual, was ready with his ad-ribs—Don claims only one person ever objected to his needling: "I made fun of a ringsider's beard and I almost got belted. That broad had no sense of humor." Now he was answering his hecklers:

To Ernest Borgnine: "Oh my God—look at you. Anybody else hurt in the accident?"

To Phil Harris: "He taught Dean Martin every drink he knows."

To Orson Welles: "Who makes your tents?"

To Johnny Carson: "The things he does for his friends can be counted on his little finger."

To Burt Lancaster: "Your career's in trouble—your curls aren't lying right anymore."

To Jim Arness: "You've got me worried, Jim. Lately when you kiss your horse I'm beginning to think you mean it."

To Liberace: "He's trying to look inconspicuous. He's the fellow in the sequined jacket and the candelabra in his mouth."

To Bob Hope: "He's so popular, when he was in Vietnam they were shooting at him from both sides."

To Freddie Prinze: "This Puerto Rican kid did a lot of good for this city, the trouble is he did it in my neighborhood."

To Sinatra: "I hear you declared war on Australia."

To Desi and Lucy: "You're more popular than Hitler and Eva Braun."

Only Desi and Lucy never got a chance to answer anybody. They never even took a bow. Berle was never funnier or more devastating: "Lucy balls Desi if she can find him." Art Linkletter, who was the roastmaster, called them the greatest team since Sacco and Vanzetti. Harry Einstein, better known as Parkyakarkus of the Eddie Cantor Show, was given the last spot before the guests of honor. He followed Berle and was only sensational. It was the spot he had asked for and he was really a hit.

Parkyakarkus walked back to his seat on the dais next to Berle. They were still applauding. He stood up to take another bow. He sat down and put his head on Milton's shoulder. They were still cheering. Linkletter asked him to get up again but he had taken his last bow.

There were at least a dozen famous doctors in the audience. When Berle shouted, "Is there a doctor in the house?" everybody thought it was a gag at first. Suddenly it hit them that something had happened. By the time the doctors made it to the dais it was too late. Parky was gone. And so was the dinner. Lucy and Desi never had a chance to even say thanks.

If the Friars who went West made a load of money for the Motion Picture Actors' Home and so many other charities, they also did pretty good for themselves. Bob Hope made so much money he keeps it on microfilm. *Fortune* magazine claimed he had 500 million or more. I asked him about that. He said: "That's ridiculous, they talk like I'm a multimillionaire. It's silly, the most I got is $27 million besides my real estate, and I have to work hard all year to pay for that. Do you know it costs me $3 million a year in taxes to pay for my holdings?"

Bing Crosby became so rich he sent care packages to Howard Hughes and Nelson Rockefeller. Rudy Vallee is so loaded he has bookends for his bankbooks. Groucho has so much bread the finance company owes *him* money. Jimmy Durante has wall-to-wall carpeting in his swimming pool. Lou Holtz who married when he was past seventy and has two children to prove it is so rich now he has an unlisted wife.

George Burns has millions but he would give a half inch of fifties if you let him sing someplace or reminisce. He has never forgotten when he was Nat Birnbaum and seven years old and living on the Lower East Side: "Every year Spiegel-Cooper, the department store people, would throw a picnic for some church in the neighborhood. Columbia Street, where we lived, was mostly Jewish. There was a Presbyterian church on the street so four of us made out we were Presbyterians. We went to the picnic and we won Ingersoll watches for being the best quartet at the picnic.

"I got home and told my mother, 'Mom, I don't want to be a Jew anymore.' She looks at me like I'm crazy, so I explained to her. I tell her, 'Mom, I've been a Jew for seven years and I got nothing to show for it. I'm a Presbyterian for one day, I got a watch.' "

At eighty he now talks about the importance of having something to get you up and out in the morning. "My work gets me going. I get out of bed because I've got a bridge game to play with friends at the club or an interesting girl can still get me out of bed." Somehow I find it interesting that when you're eighty a girl will get you *out* of bed.

Eddie Cantor left millions to his family and various charities. Ted Lewis left millions. Jack Benny lived extravagantly all his life and still he left about eight or ten big ones.

On the other hand there are some who pushed Westward Ho! and wound up with the nouveau poor: Joe Frisco whose marriage to a lady who had a few was all that enabled him to support the bookies in the manner to which he was periodically accustomed, Phil Baker, George Raft, Mickey Rooney who went bankrupt, Robert Taylor who revealed in his last years that he was "definitely not financially secure."

The great Flo Ziegfeld passed away without a bundle to remember him by; Producer George White didn't wind up with enough to produce a good meal. Champ Joe Louis couldn't pay his taxes, champ Tony Canzoneri left an estate of $21, champs Barney Ross, Slapsie Maxie, and Beau Jack, who wound up shining shoes, "kissed every buck they blew." Jessel himself is not exactly loaded.

Spending isn't just a man's disease, either. A few headlines ago we all read how Veronica Lake was working as a waitress, Denise Darcel had filed a bankruptcy petition, Mae Murray wasn't exactly flush, and Ziegfeld star Ann Pennington who originated "The Black Bottom" was flat out.

We know Harry Richman was on the dole for years from great old pals like Sinatra, New Orleans's Seymour Weiss, and New York's Ben Marden. Some of us know that Francis X. Bushman made 6 million dollars disappear between 1915 and 1919 . . . back in the days when "taxes" was just a word in Webster. But these are all B-movie plots compared to Bud Abbott. The Academy Award goes to Friar Bud Abbott.

In 1942 he and Lou Costello constituted the world's number one box-office attraction. Their movie take alone was $10 million exclusive of TV, personals, and those etceteras that add another few. They were on the Top Ten through 1952.

After that Abbott and his wife existed on Social Security. At first he refused it. ("I figured it was charity, but friends insisted, and I tell you it was a great thing.") He was getting $108 a month, his wife $44.

"I always handled my own dough," said Bud. "Jeez, if I'd have been smart I could've owned Universal Pictures."

I visited Betty and Bud in the little home they moved into in 1960. It was a half hour and a whole lifetime removed from movieville's caviar belt where they'd once set up light housekeeping in seventeen rooms. Friar Bud Abbott, who began in burlesque over half a century earlier, was receiving in a robe and slippers like any other vaudeville pro after the show was over. He was watching TV. It was 11 A.M.

I wondered what made some of these all-time big-timers blow it all. I learned the Abbotts barreled around the globe a few times. They had yachts and boarded and fed dozens of freeloaders and bought furs even the animals didn't know about. But I also learned what really depleted Friar Bud Abbott. It was his hobby.

He was an amateur magician. He could make $50,000 cash disappear in one crap game. He played poker with $7,000 pots. He'd bet a hundred on every card at blackjack. He played five-bucks-a-point gin. If a nag ran in Siberia, Uncle Buddy had something on him. As Bud put it, "I had a little piece of every action."

A friend remembers how Abbott met a "messenger" at a TV rehearsal and peeled off twenty-five $1,000 bills into his hand. The guy said, "Thanks." Abbott yawned, "Okay, kid." No tears, no remorse, no nothin'. Only a little glow of excitement that he'd risen to where he could drop twenty-five Big Ones.

Explained Bud who kind of summed it up for every vaudevillian alive or dead, loaded or busted: "Until I was forty I struggled. Five bucks to me was a fortune. So, when suddenly you have everything you don't stop to think about a rainy day. Your whole life's been rainy. All you want to think about are those sunny days.

"In burlesque I'd save up $500 during a season. Betty and I would rent a little bungalow, play a little cards with the neighboring folks, and when we hit our last deuce we'd hop back to Minsky's. So it was the same later. Only on a larger scale."

Bud Abbott's last move was to the Motion Picture Actors' Home. I wondered if he had any regrets. He had only one. That he never learned to drive. With his six Cadillacs and chauffeur gone he had to depend on friends to take him around. "Relying on people isn't my speed," he complained, "I'm not accustomed to it."

"Yeah, well, anyhow," said Betty Abbott, grinning in retrospect, "you got to admit, Bud, we useta show 'em, didn't we?"

"Yeah," smiled Friar Bud Abbott, "we useta show 'em."

And, so, we're right back at the starting line. Is it better to be like Lucille Ball, John Wayne, Burt Lancaster, Paul Anka, Raymond Burr, David Niven, Guy Lombardo, Sophia Loren, Morey Amsterdam, Milton Berle, and Cindy Adams and sock it away so you can have a comfortable old age or is it better to blow it away so you can have a swingin' young age? The subject might best be wrapped up by Groucho Marx. At Chico's funeral Groucho made the following statement: "He's the only one of the Marx Brothers who didn't save his money. He died broke. But you know something? He enjoyed his life more than any of us."

10

The Cardroom

The cardroom has ruined more actors and producers than the critics. Clive Barnes at his ugliest couldn't depress a Mike Todd, Phil Silvers, Chico or Zeppo Marx, Tony Martin, Phil Spitalny, or Lou Walters as much as an opponent hollering "Gin."

Even the million dollar gambling scandal at the Friars Club of California didn't stop them from appearing at their regular places at the green felt tables. As Phil Silvers put it before he was picked clean, "Where else can you go? It's the only game in town." Those hot rods in California who were grabbed for cheating their fellow-Friars never realized they didn't need all those intricate card-cheating gimmicks to beat the actors facing them—all they had to do was sit them out. To an actor money isn't everything—in fact, if they stay at the tables long enough, it's nothing.

Those cardrooms created a whole new class of people—the nouveau poor. Mike Todd, who produced *Around the World in 80 Days*, and Lou Walters, who owned the Latin Quarter nightclub, were capable of losing their shows or clubs at one hot session. It's been rumored Todd's *Around the World in 80 Days* and Walters's Latin Quarter sometimes changed hands on the flip of a card. Even Barbara Walters, who made $400,000 a year on NBC and millions on ABC couldn't equalize those losses and Mike Todd's missus, Elizabeth Taylor, would never have enough diamonds to satisfy his appetite at the gambling tables. Nobody could put enough in the pot to get guys like them even.

Phil Silvers made it the hard way from top banana in burlesque to Sergeant Bilco on TV, but he lost it all the easy way at the crap tables and the card tables. He is known to have blown a series, a family, and a hectic social life—all because he likes to bet. Phil admitted: "Las Vegas set me back ten days socially and five years financially." Discussing the fact that Howard Hughes, who owned a good piece of Las Vegas, never left his room, Phil cracked, "If I did that in Vegas I'd still have money too."

If a man has the fever he will gamble no matter how the cards are stacked. Phil Spitalny got beat out of a flush and his home at one sitting. When Abbott and Costello made the big time they were getting $50,000 a week and 10 percent went to their agent and 90 percent to their bookmaker. Bud Abbott admits he even went to a psychiatrist to cure his gambling on the ponies: "I used to go to the racetrack every day—now I only go when it's open."

Joe E. Lewis used to say, "No horse can go as fast as the money I bet on him but what the hell can I do with the money? I'll only blow it on the government anyway." And then there's the actor who just made mental bets—he lost his mind.

The Friars may be a wonderful place to meet your agent or the producer who could throw you your next big part, but you're taking a chance if you see them when they're in a card game. I know—I found out the hard way. I had heard of a part that was perfect for me in *Star and Garter*, which Mike Todd was producing. I couldn't make personal contact with him at the theatre so I asked my friend, Benny Fields, the minstrel, to say a good word for me.

Benny did better than that. He took me by the hand to the club where Mike was having his daily battle with Lou Walters. Mike was very nice because of my sponsor but, of course, he couldn't stop dealing just to listen to me! I discussed the part while he dealt the cards and for a while there I really thought I had it all sewed up. Everything was gorgeous until Lou hollered excitedly, "What's the name of the game?" I answered, "Gin." Mike forgot to break his kings and I was out of the show and out of the club in two minutes.

Mike, like all gamblers, was an easy touch when he was on a winning streak. When Al Lackey, who was married to Sophie Tucker, couldn't pay her rent at the Edison Hotel, Mike took Al to the manager, paid the bill, threw in a couple of weeks in advance, and even gave him a few in his kick to feel the part.

You know, naturally, that Al blew the money by a nose in the third at Santa Anita. That night he trudged to the club to see if he could recoup. Todd was playing gin with the club champ, songwriter Benny Davis. "Can I have another fifty?" he asked Mike. "I promise I'll give it back as soon as I hear from Soph." Todd slipped him half a C-note and Lackey immediately went to the other side of the table and laid it on Benny Davis against Todd.

I don't want you to get the impression from all this that the Friars are responsible for show people losing their money. Show people don't need any help in that department. They do it pretty good by themselves—and not necessarily by gambling.

Broads and booze, in that order, successfully vacuumed up the assets of a Georgie Jessel or a Harry Richman faster than they could make it. Jessel and Richman never put a dollar bet down on anything—never were devotees of a cardroom—but they laid their fortunes down on broads of every race, creed, color, and bust measurement ever since they first found out there was a difference between blue booties and pink booties.

It's interesting about Georgie and Harry and the other antique Lotharios like Groucho and George Burns in that the older they get the younger their girls. Truth is, they still chase girls, only now it has to be down hill. Burns has tuxedos that are older than the females he dates. He often doesn't know whether to feed them or burp them. Burns at least admits he's taking a memory course and he dosen't mind paying for the lessons.

Georgie Jessel, a rugged roué who has been the alcoholic playmate of the famous as well as the infamous, is an aged blend—actor, lover, orator, comedian. He has the most beautiful flow of the English language—and his flow of Scotch isn't bad either.

Jessel is one of a kind. It cost him $200,000 for one night with a girl in his beach house and he's proud of it. It's what he had to pay in a paternity suit for this single night of pleasure. When the judge decided he was the father, Georgie beamed: "Your honor, I want to thank you for this compliment. I will, at my advanced age, accept your decision with pride." This was in 1961. Jessel was sixty-three at the time. Georgie says he has never taken a girl to his beach house since. Now he goes to *their* houses and lets *their* lawyers worry. His latest just came out of summer camp and he's very proud of her. She just made Eagle Scout.

In his autobiography Georgie reminisces about his love life with everybody from his three wives, Norma Talmadge, Florence Courtney, and Lois Andrews to Rita Hayworth, Pola Negri, and the Happy Hooker, Xaviera Hollander. If Jessel did all the things he claims, they would stuff him in a bottle on a shelf in Harvard.

Georgie is a romantic. If it's a ten-dollar hustler, he'll send her flowers, pick her up in a limousine, take her to the finest restaurant, and give her a piece of jewelry besides. On top of that he still pays the fee. He ends up paying $400 or $500 for the same thing he would have gotten for ten bucks.

That's why he was very proud when Xaviera Hollander introduced herself to him in a Chinese restaurant and offered to pick up his check. He says with the Happy Hooker it was like going to school all over again. She taught him a few things even he didn't know—and he thought he had graduated a long time ago. She told him, "It's a pleasure with you—not business."

Jessel was proud of his Happy Hooker and schlepped her everywhere. It wasn't unusual to see Georgie and Xaviera sitting at a prominent table for two at 21—each waving to their respective fans.

About Xaviera, Jessel says, "She is the most gifted woman in a bedroom I have ever experienced." Oddly enough, this was the only member of the opposite sex who didn't cost him any money.

I love Jack Benny's line. He said, "This year alone Georgie Jessel personally supported 1,250,000 Jews in Israel—and 325 chorus girls in the United States."

Jessel could spend as much on a girl as Mike Todd could on a night of gin. A lot of years back he chartered a plane to fly him from Cleveland to New York because he had a date with Faye Emerson who had just broken up with Elliott Roosevelt. No commercial airline could get him in on time so he spent $2,500 to keep his date with Faye. I was on the same bill with him so I was invited to take the trip back.

We were laughing and talking on the flight to LaGuardia. He was talking and I was laughing. Due to the low ceiling we couldn't land and kept circling for more than an hour. Tension mounted and conversation in the plane ceased. Soon all that could be heard was the steady drone of the motors. "My luck," I mumbled, "we'll get killed and you'll get top billing."

Not a sound. Not a word. Not even a nod from my seatmate. I didn't think he had heard me. Twenty minutes later when we were finally safe on the ground Jessel laughed, "That was very funny what you said up there—about me getting top billing—tell that to Faye when we meet her."

Jackie Gleason was another booze and broad man who lived like a Sybarite even before he had it. He would borrow fifty or a hundred bucks from me and then take me out on the town with the girl of the moment and pay me back when he had it.

Mickey Rooney spent his loot on seven wives. Earl Carroll, George White, and Florenz Ziegfeld on wine, women, and show business. But "you ain't heard nothin' yet" till you hear the saga of singer Harry Richman—the biggest spender of them all. He made Howard Hughes, Diamond Jim Brady, and Tommy Manville look like they were on relief.

To impress a girl, Richman would tip the waiter $50 just to get a menu. It is reliably reported he said to the maître d' at the Stork Club, "What's the biggest tip you ever received?" The headwaiter replied "$100." Harry gave him $200 and then asked, "Now tell me—who gave you the hundred?" and the man at the door said, "You did, Mr. Richman."

Harry always had an assortment of mink, sable, and chinchilla coats in his closets in case a *kurveh* deserved it. He would buy a dozen diamond bracelets at a time on the chance that he'd run into a beauty or a young one—or a young beauty. He only worked to attract gorgeous women around him. He was a sucker for a sad story or a beautiful girl. Almost every night he would walk into the most expensive joints in town with a girl to match on each arm, and blow the whole bankroll.

Harry Richman was a pilot, an amateur boxer, a fisherman of record, a star, a lover of note, and the greatest party giver of all time. His friends were the millionaires as well as the gangsters, athletes, authors, the most obliging ladies in the world, presidents, ambassadors, royalty, and Bowery bums—and Richman was always the host.

Harry drank too much, gambled too much, and played too much —but as he said proudly, even when he was completely broke, "It was a hell of a life." When we realized he didn't know where the next booking or the next meal was coming from, his buddies decided to run a benefit for him. I came to him with the news while he was in the hospital. "Besides that, Sinatra, Tony Martin, and Hy Gardner are working on a TV and record deal for you," I told him. "They are going to get the greatest singing stars in America and Europe to sing the songs you introduced and all the profits go to you. It could be as much as a quarter of a million dollars." Harry said simply, "That's nice."

I said, "Tell me, Harry, how would you like to invest all this money? What will you do with it?" "I'll blow it on the biggest party the world has ever seen," he answered.

There nonetheless remains that segment of humanity who does not recognize that a hot broad on your chest has got to be better than three lays in your hand any day. These are the humans who are suffering from a terminal case of gambling fever. It's not that they don't like to live big. It's not that they don't like to love big. It's just that they've done it already. They've been there and back. The way they play at chasing women there's no element of chance. To them women are a sure thing. The only odds left, the only risks still remaining for them to take, the only way in which they can yet pit their skills lies in gambling. Therefore, a triple schneid is the only score these guys are really excited about making.

Enter stage center the cardroom of The Friars. The Friars wasn't different from any other social club or golf club late in the day or swimming club when it's raining. They played cards the same as they did in Akron or Santa Fe. Only here the players were more famous. Instead of the local butcher, it was an international celebrity. The stakes weren't bigger—only the names were bigger.

A series of losses and a couple of million dollars later, the governors with the help of Carl Timin, the executive director, and his assistant at the time, Walter Goldstein, decided to deemphasize gambling and bring it back to the social club and meeting place of show people it was intended to be.

They directed the big gamblers to go peddle their horses someplace else. They booed the high rollers and it was back to penny gin and one dollar poker limits. The same thing went for pinochle, klabiash, and bridge. They posted signs that spelled it all out. The cardrooms used to seat a hundred people and they were always filled—sometimes two sessions a night—and with two dollars per chair and a dollar and a half for cards that could mean about $50,000 a year for the club. As Walter Goldstein put it, "We now lose money in the cardrooms, but our members are saving theirs."

Ironically enough, all this happened in 1957—about five years before the million dollar gambling sting at the California Friars Club.

The Friars Club of California is a two-story, mustard-colored job that decorates Santa Monica Boulevard in Beverly Hills's high rent district. It has no windows, the better not to see such exalted comers as Dean Martin, Sinatra, Tony Martin, Phil Silvers, Zeppo Marx, millionaire shoe manufacturer Harry Karl who was a once-upon-a-time husband of Debbie Reynolds, millionaire camera manufacturer Ted Briskin who was a once-upon-a-time husband of Betty Hutton, honorary Friar Ronald Reagan, and on up and down the social, theatrical, and financial level.

As befitting the membership, the decor is early opulent. Private underground garage, enormous lush dining room, ankle-deep rugs with the logo—a circle surrounding the poodle-clipped head of a friendly fat Friar, colored photos of famous Friars (the theatrical kind not the clerical kind), and an upstairs cardroom with a private key, and assorted shapes of green felt tables for poker, pinochle, and two- or four-handed gin rummy.

Seems that in 1962, the afternoon of June 28, a little double-dealing took place. Harry Karl, fiftyish, gray-haired, nice looking, expensively dressed, and a super gin-rummy player said bye-bye to his wife, Debbie Reynolds, and drove to the club. Tony Martin kissed his gorgeous wife, Cyd Charisse, bye-bye also and he, too, went to the club to be a second to Harry Karl. Then there was another guy, a real-estate wheeler dealer from Vegas. Who he kissed good-bye I don't know, but on account of his wheeling and dealing at the gin-rummy table Harry Karl kissed good-bye to $18,000.

As has since been written about, documented by the FBI, testified to in hearings, and known to us all, the Cheat, in the person of a Las Vegas real-estate man, had thoughtfully arranged a little insurance in the form of a peephole in the ceiling above plus an accomplice with an eyeball in the peephole and a finger in a short-wave outfit whose signals were received on a transistor taped to the Cheat's ample belly.

The operation was ingenious. The peephole was covered with an air vent painted to match the ceiling. An optical lens brought the pigeon's cards into the 20/20 vision of the bug-eyed accomplice. When the Cheat fingered a discard the Accomplice would beep. It was a sort of one-if-by-land-two-if-by-sea signal. In other words, two beeps against the Cheat's belly meant yes, one meant uh-uh. When the Cheat wanted to knock he'd signal with his thumb, the responding buzzer on the belly button gave the answer.

The first little practice session had lasted thirteen hours. Over the next year Harry Karl's status as a pigeon widened to include Ted Briskin. As we understand it they lost in one month something in the neighborhood of $100,000, which is a pretty classy neighborhood for anybody. Harry Karl paid in cash from a shopping bag filled with small bills. Briskin paid by check. But pay they both did. Karl lost in total about $80,000, Briskin $200,000.

With the help of another accomplice or three or four or five, the pigeon coop extended to Tony Martin who went for $10,000, Groucho's brother Zeppo whose donation came to something like $6,000, superagent Kurt Frings who dropped nearly $25,000, Phil Silvers who was hit too badly to even say. As the list of suckers widened so did the list of suckees. It went far beyond the original group of finks. The record has it that when the big, big money began dropping, the bad guys who were then pulling the strings were definitely not amateurs. They were professionals otherwise known as hoods, the pros who wear black hats. The take came to roughly a million dollars.

A little suspicion mixed with a little bad blood stirred together with a whole lot of lousy feelings and a pinch of greed eventually brought the roof down. Two dozen lawmen were dispatched to bring in the evidence, and six years later the government brought its case to trial.

The Beverly Hills municipal code and the California penal code make gambling punishable by a fine or a vacation behind bars. A nonprofit charitable private club, however, nullifies this little irritation. Speaking about policing the situation, the former chief of police of Beverly Hills, Clinton Anderson, said, "You have to have evidence and a search warrant. We know there's card-playing there and we suspected there was gambling going on there. But we never received a complaint." Former Chief Anderson is also an honorary Friar.

Today everybody in the mustard-colored job on Santa Monica Boulevard is very circumspect. Today those who still have access to the secret place of the most high—the locked cardrooms on the third floor—have a private key. Today the Friars of California has an ethics committee. Today they bar anybody who even smells undesirable. Today the members guarantee all is back to brotherhood and friendship and one-for-all-and-all-for-one and charitable works and small but friendly card games.

Prae omnia fraternitas.

11

Burns and Benny
Benny and Burns

One year the club had a double header. In tandem they gave it to the Damon and Pythias of comedy, Jack Benny and George Burns. This time there was no discussion of who was the headliner. Each wanted the other to get top billing.

"It's a good thing you didn't wait any longer to have this dinner," George Burns, seventy-six, cracked. "We're at a peculiar age. The other night Jack and I went to see a porno picture—and we fell asleep." Like always, they took Jack out with laugh cramps at what his pal of fifty-five years said.

Their entire lives were built on laughter. It kept them alive and young. When Benny celebrated his eightieth birthday on Valentine's Day, 1974, he noted: "I believe I'm only fifty years old. I walk the same, talk the same, there's hardly been any change in me over the years. I suppose you should be glad when you reach a certain age—but then again, it's an age when you say, "How much more do I have?"

George Burns, who knew Benny pre-Mary Livingstone, said, "He's the nicest, kindest, most considerate, generous person I have ever known. If I had been a toe dancer, Mary Benny would have had competition.

"You know, you can be only thirty-five years, but if your first joke doesn't get a laugh, you get to be eighty in a hurry! And if you're eighty and you get laughs in a hurry, then you get to be thirty—Jack will always be thirty."

The Jack Benny-George Burns fairy tale came alive at the Americana Hotel on May 13, 1972. It was a fairy tale, too, for the assorted charities who shared $195,000 from this largest of all blue plates.

Oddly enough, this dinner almost didn't come off.

The Friars were scratching around desperately for a guest of honor. "How are we going to top the last three big ones?" Executive Director Walter Goldstein moaned to anybody who'd listen. "Barbra Streisand in '69, Tom Jones in '70, Alan King in '71—only God can top it—and he's not available—*Who?* Who?"

"Why don't we get Jesse Block to help?" Walter's assistant, Jean-Pierre, suggested. "He saved us in 1951 with Jack Benny, Bob Hope in 1952, Jessel in 1954—if we can't get God—let's get the Savior. He's a great Friar, he'll come up with something."

In the old days when Jesse Block and Eve Sully were the royalty of vaudeville, they trouped and tanked with Jack Benny and Mary Livingstone, George Burns and Gracie Allen, Ida and Eddie Cantor, Benny Fields and Blossom Seeley, and that whole lineup of young acts who went on to become paragraphs in *Who's Who.*

Jesse, a rich, retired stockbroker who held onto his friends as well as his money, hasn't had the greasepaint on in twenty-five years or more, but he's still everybody's pal and all he has to do is call in the IOUs.

Walter laid it on the table for Jesse. "We have to feed the kitty that Joe E. Lewis left in his will for indigent actors. We've used most of his $50,000 plus the Ted Lewis grant. We need funds to send the Friars Hospital Frolics to institutions and hospitals and to send our troupes of minstrels into old-age homes to bring a little cheer and love and to support our project Santa Claus where we give away gifts, food, and clothes every Christmas."

"I know all that," Jesse said, "so what do you want me to do?"

"Get us a guest of honor—one of your pals—Benny, Burns, Hope."

"I'll try."

"We've never had a flop," Walter said, "starting in 1916 when the Friars Frolic was for the benefit of the Actors' Fund of America at the old Hippodrome, an event that was so successful that the show went on the road with nineteen performers in fifteen cities and brought a net gain of $55,311."

"Okay, Okay," Jesse said, "I'll do it, I'll . . ."

"Remember," Walter continued, "we've had the greatest guests of honor—Oscar Hammerstein, David Belasco, Irving Berlin, George M. Cohan, Enrico Caruso, Mayor Jimmy Walker . . ."

"Hey, remember me?" grinned Jesse. "I've been executive chairman of entertainment of this club for a hundred years! I don't know what I'll come up with but I'll come up with something. Let me go to work."

George Burns was the first to turn it down. "I'd like to do it for you and the Friars and George M. Cohan," he said, "but who's going to come to see me these days? I don't want to give you your first flop." Through clouds of his own cigar smoke Burns said, "I'll tell you something about George M. Cohan. He'd only pal around with actors who had no talent—I was one of his closest friends." A few more cigar puffs then, "Listen, why don't you get Jack Benny? Now there is a guy who will pack the joint for you."

Benny refused for the same modest reason: "Will Rogers once said, 'They never give you a dinner until you can afford to buy one'—well, I can afford to buy my own dinner and I don't want to louse up yours."

Just when Walter was ready to lock himself in the steam room and never come out, Jesse came up with the idea: "How about Burns *and* Benny—154 years of comedy. They'll do it for each other and for me. I'll fly out to California and talk to them."

"Great," Walter agreed, "it'll be the three Bs—Block, Benny, and Burns."

"Now if I can only convince them . . ."

The good news came just before Christmas in 1971, just before Walter was going to hang himself on his Christmas tree. Benny and Burns accepted.

"Now what will we do about a toastmaster?" Walter fretted, wringing his hands anew.

Bob Hope was scheduled to be in Hawaii, Milton Berle was booked solid for that month, I think I had a Bar Mitzvah or something in Brooklyn, Groucho and Jessel weren't available. Joey Bishop said okay and they were on their way. Only it's never that easy.

The Grand Ballroom of the Waldorf was a proper home for years, but it was felt that this event could dredge out maybe two thousand people so they needed a larger space. The next headache was to locate a bigger place. After investigating east side, west side, and all around the town the decision was the Americana Hotel. The next problem was to coordinate everything and fasten on a particular night suitable to everybody. Eventually the date was set for May 14.

"Let's go," Walter hollered, "call the printer! call the staff! call

The George Burns–Jack Benny dinner with roastmasters Art Linkletter and Jesse Block.

the officers and board of governors! Let's set up the committees, we only have a few months. The stationery alone takes a month!"

Immediately the letters went out to a couple of hundred famous personalities around the world requesting permission to list them on the honorary committee while at the same time Jesse Block sent wires to the top names in show business to grace the dais. This is palm-sweating time because you can't print the stationery until you get an okay from everybody.

The stationery arrived the first week in February. The paper glittered with the solid gold names linked to it. Bob Hope was on as honorary chairman and so were all the names of his glossy honorary committee. The stationery featured the pictures of George Burns and Jack Benny on top, with the legend "May 14, 1972. Grand Ballroom, Americana Hotel."

The gift package arrangement committee was set, the public relations committee was set, Al Massler, the chairman of the program committee, was set. Everything was set. Everything became unset. In the middle of one night Jesse was curled up in his bed in the Essex House in New York happily dreaming of ecstatic things like the morning *after* the dinner when the phone rang. It was Jack Benny from California. He didn't realize the Emmys were on that same night as the dinner and can we change the night of the dinner?

Under the circumstances Jesse did the only intelligent thing. He sat bolt upright in bed and figured what the hell . . . why should he be up while Goldstein is asleep. In brotherly Friarly fraternal good fellowship Jesse dialed Walter. Walter naturally celebrated this good news by staying up the rest of the night, too. I mean, who can worry when you're sleeping, right?

Early and bleary the following morning the first order of business was to con the heavily booked hotel into changing to a night earlier—May 13. After a four-way conversation with the hoteliers, Jack Benny, Jesse Block, and Walter this was accomplished. What was also accomplished was that everybody lost a little piece of lung and a little piece of their liver getting this accomplished. The remaining part was easy: just informing the dais guests, some of whom now could not make it and some of whom were annoyed because they'd already shifted their engagements to be able to make it in the first place and some of whom were programmed to always make it look like it was not that easy to get them whenever you wanted them. Then the toastmaster had to be informed and, naturally, he was out of town and had to be tracked down. And then it was merely a question of informing the printer who immediately upped the price because he had done it at "such a low cost the first time that I lost money" and then getting new stationery and then and then and then . . . .

Now for the good news. Sinatra accepted and he's going to sing a song with a special lyric by Sammy Cahn. Cary Grant said yes and will sit on the dais along with Claudette Colbert, Helen Hayes, Dinah Shore, Burt Reynolds, Art Linkletter, Garson Kanin, Lillian Gish, Neil Simon, Paul Anka, Barbara Walters, Phil Silvers, and our goodwill ambassador Pearl Bailey. A personal hype by Jesse to Mary Livingstone Benny to make this rare personal appearance and she too was billed on the dais as an extra added attraction.

Jesse and Walter immediately went into hiding from everybody who demanded good seat locations. Walter settled the whole thing by appointing a seating committee which came equipped with a double-parked getaway car which hustled them to a plane which left for Bali right after the baked Alaska was served. Next to a leper the worst thing to be is a member of the seating committee. It is a 100 percent thankless job. Suddenly the people who never part with a dime to a blind beggar creep out of the woodwork and spring for two tickets and demand front seats. Suddenly every human being you ever met is either hard of hearing or hard of seeing or has to sit right in front "because I'm such a good friend of George and Jack that they'll be looking for me the whole night to catch my eye."

The battle was over but the daily skirmishes had just begun. Nailing Friar Ray Bloch and his orchestra to play for the show and dancing and Friar Dick Jacobs to do the orchestrations and Friar Eli Basse to write the special material and the Friars Ensemble to warble the Victor Herbert-Charles Emerson Cook club song also can't be done with mirrors.

Next on the Hit Parade of aggravations were the gifts. "Gifts," chanted Walter, running around. "Gifts. I need gifts for the dais, gifts for the guests of honor. Gifts. I need gifts." Trucks with 142 crates of gifts somehow found their way to the hotel. And what good are gifts without security, right? Now they needed security for all the equipment and all the gifts and what good is it to keep 2,000 sample giveaway bottles of perfume safe if somebody decides to hijack a Burt Reynolds, so more security was laid on for the famous guests and all in all a busy time was had by all.

The revenue realized from the evening was to be divided among Benny's favorite, Share, Inc., an organization in California that helps youngsters who can't help themselves, George's selection of the City of Hope, and Jesse's choice of the Will Rogers Memorial Hospital. A hundred and ninety-five thousand can bring a lot of goodies to a lot of people.

A day before the dinner lucky Jesse got a couple of calls that started the ulcers at full speed again. Alan King has a family emergency and can't make it and Jessel is laid up with a croup or a *kurveh* or something but the point is he's out flat. Walter and Jesse are back on the phone all day for replacements. Jesse finally buttons up Pat Henry and David Frost who promise to show.

"Well," Jesse sighs to Walter, "it was a tough fight but we made it. It looks like we got a real winner."

"Yeah," Walter nods, "but who will we get for next year?"

119

And so the Friars honored the odd couple of the Geritol Set—Jack Benny and George Burns. Art Linkletter called them the "Geritol Junkies."

Columnist Irv Kupcinet of the *Chicago Sun-Times* was lovingly sentimental as he addressed them: "God bless your hearts and any other living organ." Cary Grant explained why George only dated young girls: "At his age it gets increasingly difficult to find any that are older."

Jesse Block read a telegram from Bob Hope, the honorary chairman. Jesse said: "Bob would have been here but he knows Jack and George love each other and all their friends like Helen Hayes and Lillian Gish, Claudette Colbert, Ruth Gordon, Dinah Shore, and Ed Sullivan would be around—and he likes to go where there are wars. He sent this telegram: 'Dear Jesse—try to make it an early dinner or these two guys will fall asleep on the dais.'"

George Burns prepared for the dinner. He called ahead of time to order his favorite dish—scrambled eggs and ketchup. This was really living for George—at his age cream of wheat is spicy. Jack only asked that they pick up the check.

The double-sword ceremony started when Abbot Ed Sullivan introduced Toastmaster Joey Bishop to start the "Big Big Shew."

Joey wasted no laughs: "I wanna know one thing. Why are we in New York honoring two guys who live in Beverly Hills? I think the right thing would have been to take these guys and honor them where their friends are—the Will Rogers old-age home.

"I don't know why the Friars couldn't have gotten one big name instead of two seminames. You got one guy who can't sing—another guy who can't play a fiddle. If you were going to honor somebody without talent, why didn't you honor me?

"Actually we're here tonight to pay tribute to these two senile misfits. One big name would have solved the whole thing. George Burns still considers himself a swinger. He's got a water bed filled with Kaopectate. Only he's a little upset tonight. He got a 'Dear John' letter from Moms Mabley.

"These are the two dearest friends in all of show business. And if you're ever in Beverly Hills and you go to the Hillcrest Country Club, it's a thrill to watch each one of them massaging the other guy's heart. It's one of the all-time big thrills you'll ever see."

Nothing is sacred at these roasts. At one dinner for Pearl Bailey I was the roastmaster. I explained to her before we started that

I couldn't possibly attack her—she's black, she's a woman over fifty, married to a white man, a goodwill ambassador for our country . . . She said: "If you spare the rod—I'll never forgive you. If I can dish it out, I can take it." Pearl laughed the loudest when I said about her: "This is a classy girl, this Pearl Bailey. When she didn't get the picture for *Hello, Dolly!*, she made no fuss—Ginger Rogers cried—Carol Channing whimpered—but not a word from Pearl—she did have the boys from the NAACP do a little picketing."

Now Joey Bishop wasn't sparing the rod—there were no sacred cows: "They sent me these two ladies to introduce—Lillian Gish and Helen Hayes—I never heard such cursing from two broads in my life."

He introduced Art Linkletter as "a gentleman who made a fortune by putting children on his lap and talking to them. I got an uncle did the same thing—he's now serving ten to twenty."

Art Linkletter was nostalgic: "We're old enough to remember, George, Jack, and I, when hot pants was a condition. We recall that when there was no pill the best method of birth control was a rusty zipper.

Jack Benny's bookends are Senator Jacob Javits and Joan Crawford.

"These new stars like Burt Reynolds, who is here tonight, can't compare to guys like Benny and Burns! Big sex symbol. I looked it up in Funk & Wagnalls and it says 'a symbol is a substitute for the real thing.' I saw Reynolds in that centerfold—it was the first centerfold that really folds out. Now George Burns was asked to pose for one of those same pictures but he had to refuse—because he only has two hands."

Linkletter said he was delighted when Jesse Block's letter was forwarded to him in Korea for this dinner: "I couldn't believe a letter would come from New York from the Friars Club to where I was in Asia. But when I opened it and sniffed the familiar fragrance of cigars and chicken fat, I knew it came from the Friars Club."

Frank Sinatra was introduced by Bishop: "A lot of people didn't know Frank was in town, but I knew he was because I saw a welcome wagon being driven by four naked broads. So here he is, Frank Sinatra."

Frank said: "I'd like to say a few words about George Wallace —get in back of the bus, baby.

"Now I want to acknowledge all these lovely people on the dais and in the audience who have contributed to this lovely evening. You have contributed to this lovely evening because all of it goes to charity and that's what the whole idea is all about, that we as Friars put these on as many times a year as we can to raise money for Milton Berle, Jesse Block, and a lot of other bums who run the club. I know because I was an ex-abbot until I dipped my duke in the tambourine and they caught me one time."

Frank does and says what he wants at these parties—or anyplace else for that matter. For no reason, he told this story: "One fella says to another fella, 'Hey, baby, what would you do if you found another man making love to your wife?' He said, 'I'll shoot his goddamn Seeing Eye dog.'

"I don't know what the hell I'm doing here. Here I am retired— I've been drinking all night long with the kind of gasoline I like to drink—sitting with Cary Grant who is drinking Coke or Pepsi or Fabergé or something—this bum drinks perfume—I really don't know why I'm here—except I love these two bums—Benny and Burns."

Bishop said: "I'd like to retire the way Frank retired—boats, booze, broads—he may have to come back in the business to get some rest."

I was watching Jack and George as it came time for them to acknowledge their honors and return the compliments and gags to their pallbearers. Jack was looking over his glasses looking at his notes, George was puffing double-time on his cigar so that by now the dais looked like a foggy night in London town.

These dinners are always nervous-making time for those on the dais. It's not really a show—it's an audition is what it is—for anybody who gets up to the microphone. It doesn't matter how big or how small you are—you have to be good. You have a whole career riding on this freebie. Only the strong in heart and stomach can take it—or dish it out.

Take the story of Claudette Colbert. It took Jesse half a dozen phone calls to convince her she was wanted and was still as popular as ever and Jack Benny asked for her and she would be sitting next to Frank Sinatra who loves her.

She couldn't have been as nervous with her first screen kiss. "All I want you to do is take a bow," Jesse pleaded. She did show up looking as beautiful and as lovely as ever—but nervous as hell—and all she was going to do was stand up and take a bow.

I watched the first lady of the American theatre, Helen Hayes, who has won every kind of award on the stage and screen, take out her compact a dozen times to make sure she looked great before she delivered her two lines.

The guys who have the toughest job are the comics. It's the greatest show on earth watching them riffle through their papers as another comic does a joke they intended to use. Now they have to eliminate that one and think of a topper—where can they find their writers at H-Hour?

It's opening night for everybody on the dais until they get that first laugh, until the hand at the end. Timing is so important. The right line at the right time. Timing, waiting for the laugh—which sometimes takes a lifetime—a dirty line that doesn't come off.

I watched nice guy Burt Reynolds, who tries to do the arrogant, bravado, nonchalant bit, throw a dirty line that almost put him into a spin. He was so nervous, he apologized to the priest on the dais and to the bishop in the audience. After that joke, he should have gone right to the pope.

All this is the overture compared to the husband or wife or agent who is in the audience. They are more nervous than any of the giants on the dais. For the spouse it means she won't be able to live with him for a month if he's a flop. For the agent it could mean the cancellation of a show or getting the blame for putting him on this benefit in the first place.

Every performer who sits on that dais is prepared. It costs a fortune to do it right—for writers, new gowns or evening clothes, arrangements, giving up paid jobs to do this for free. Why?

I sat on the dais so many times asking myself that very question. Why? What do I need it for? What the hell am I doing thinking up louse-ups for somebody I love. Why? And on top of that I could be a flop. And if I'm not a flop and I get the big laugh, I could be offending somebody that's a good friend or his family or his manager.

I was toastmaster at one dinner for a famous television host. He was really running hot. Everybody wanted to be on his show. We were pretty good friends until I said about him, "Success hasn't changed him, he's still the same arrogant bastard he always was." It got a tremendous laugh, but I haven't been on his show since.

Gene Baylos is one of the few comedians who doesn't get nervous, and he's always the biggest hit at these parties, if not the biggest name. "The only thing that bothers me," he says, "if I'm a flop I could lose the Concord Hotel for Saturday night."

"My luck," Gene says, "I'm always a big hit for free, and Milton, Alan, and Henny get the jobs. Everytime I'm a smash, which is when I appear for free, the producer or director or agent who is in the audience says, 'He's great—who does he remind you of?' And he gets the job."

These dinners are nightmares for producers and toastmasters. Jesse Block at this moment has twenty-two personalities who are sticking pins in him because they weren't invited to sit on the dais.

Then there's the entertainer who is in a hurry to get on. He says he has another show to do. The only show he has is with his wife, and he doesn't do that too good. But he wants to get the first crack at them before somebody beats him to the jokes.

One of the big problems is overbooking the dais. That's in case the biggies don't show. Now you have to invite some of the lessees who always show. Of course, with Sinatra and Dinah Shore and Pearl Bailey and Cary Grant who do show, there isn't time to put on the seminames—how do you brush it up with them? You'll need them again the next time when the biggies don't show. How does the toastmaster introduce them and keep them from getting to the microphone?

And deliver me from the politician who is there to dress up the dais and promised to just "take a bow." He is introduced and before you can say, "Glad to see you," he is at the microphone and he whips out his glasses and his ten-page script and starts to make his campaign speech.

Do you use the hook on the owner of the television station or the producer or manager who is an important part of the guest of honor's life? How do you get him off before you lose the crowd?

"You can't satisfy everybody and still do a good show. How do you tell Dinah you only want one song? Or Berle—only eight minutes. Or George, "No speeches, just introduce the guest of honor." That's why these dinners are held once a year. It takes the producer, the executive director, and the toastmaster all year to recover from one of these parties.

And now it was time for Benny Kubelsky and Nathan Birnbaum to come front and center—Jack Benny and George Burns—the greatest team since Leopold and Loeb or Sacco and Vanzetti. Those two brother Friars will now be placed in history with Abraham and Isaac, Martin and Lewis, Abercrombie and Fitch, Moscowitz and Lupowitz, Amos and Andy, Glen and Jenkins, Cain and Abel, and Damon and Pythias—there was talk about them too.

Burns and Benny were only beautiful. Burns lost the toss so he spoke first:

"Now I want to thank the Friars for giving Jack and myself this beautiful dinner and it's a good thing you didn't wait much longer. At our age, every time we sit down to eat it could be the last supper. Well, that's not true. We'll be around for a long time. We can't leave, we're both booked.

"And you know, I don't know about this old kid here, but for myself at my age, there's still a lot of things I love to do. I love to sing, I love to smoke, I love to, well I used to love to, and even when I was able, when I was able to, I always enjoyed singing and smoking more than I did that. I was never crazy about sex. When I was young, the only thing I wanted to get into was show business. I always felt that if I would, I could hurt myself and never win another Charleston contest. I was always self-conscious about, you know. Even now I'm embarrassed when I put my cigar into my holder.

"When I was eighteen or nineteen years old I wanted to sing, I wanted to dance, I wanted to be on the stage, I wanted to be an actor, and I made it, and I don't know how cause I had no talent. Nobody liked my singing, but me. I was a buck dancer but I could only tap with my right foot. I did a dramatic sketch and everybody laughed. I told jokes and nobody laughed. So I decided to become a straight man because a straight man does nothing. Figured the comedian asks the questions, the straight man, all you have to do is repeat the question and the comedian's got the punch line. He gets the laugh, tells the joke, and I'm in show business, and it worked.

"I'll never forget I had a date with a little girl once, a waitress. She invited me up to her place and we walked in there and the lights were low and the music was soft and she had on a negligee and she said, 'How would you like to have a drink?' I figured this was my chance to see if I could make it as a straight man, so I repeated the question. I said, 'How would you like to have a drink?' And she had one. Then she said, 'Would you like to have another one,' and I repeated, 'Would you like to have another one,' and she had another one. After five or six drinks she got stoned. She said, 'Why don't we go into the bedroom,' and I said, ' Why don't we go into the bedroom,' and we did and we got into bed and she says, 'Turn out the lights,' and I said, 'Turn out the lights.' She turned out the lights and I went home. She didn't get any laughs so I left. That girl nearly ruined my career.

"And you know, let me tell you something, I would do anything to stay in show business. I remember when I did a single, my name was Harry Pierce. Jesse Block was right, I used all kinds of names. My billing was Harry Pierce, 'the singer from Rhode Island in an act of Providence.' I'd never been to Rhode Island but I thought that was pretty classy billing. And somehow I was booked into the Gem Theatre on Houston Street for three days at $15, $5 a day. And that contract had a no-cancellation clause in it. In those days they could cancel you after the first performance. After doing my act I came off the stage, the manager was waiting for me in the wings, and he said, 'Look, kid, that act of yours can ruin my theatre. You're booked for three days for $15. Here's the $15 and go home.' I says, 'Not me, I'm booked for three days, I'm gonna play the three days.' He says, 'I'll give you $20, go home.' I says, 'No. All right, you didn't like my first show, I'll change my songs. I'll open with 'Tiger Girl,' and then I'll do 'In the Heart of a Cherry,' and for my third number, I'll sing 'Augusta J. McCan Was a Henpecked Married Man.' He says, 'I'll make it $25.' I says, 'No, sir, I'm staying,

I'm a performer.' He says, 'All right kid, you can stay but give me back your key to the men's room.' Which I did, which was kind of bad cause that's where I was dressing. Now let me tell you something. When you don't go to the men's room for three days it doesn't help your singing. In fact, after my second day I didn't dare to do my yodeling finish.

"I used to change my name every day. I couldn't get a job with the same name twice. I remember I was sitting in Farley Marcus's office, a small-time booking agent, and the guy came in and he says, 'Where can I find Maurice Valenti.' I said, 'I'm Maurice Valenti.' I thought I was. He gave me a contract to play the Myrtle Theatre. The contract said, 'Maurice Valenti and His Wonder Dog.' I signed it. I'd do anything to stay in show business. I got a piece of liver, I went out, I caught myself a dog. I went to the Myrtle Theatre to do my act, walked out on the stage with the dog under my arm, I stood there and sang my songs. In the middle of my third song, I used to yodel, and when I started the yodels the dog did his act. Twice. It ruined my finish, I couldn't do my sand dance.

"Now I'm going to tell you a story you're not going to believe at all. I did an act with a seal once and it wasn't my act. I was living above Winick's Restaurant on 45th Street in a boardinghouse and there was an actor living with me. His name was Betz and he did an act with a seal. It was Captain Betz and Flipper. And they booked into the Dewey Theatre on 14th Street supposed to open Monday and the guy got sick. And he asked me to take his place. I said, 'Betz, you're crazy, I never worked with a seal.' He said, 'George, there's nothing to it. The seal does the whole thing. You walk out, you're standing on the stage, the curtain goes up. The seal is on a little platform. You're standing there with a ball in your hand, and your pockets full of fish.' He says, 'You throw the ball, he throws it back to you, and you throw the seal a piece of fish and the seal applauds with his flippers. Then backstage there's a thing set up, a tightrope thing. The seal goes up the ladder, walks across the tightrope, and comes down the other ladder, again you throw the seal a piece of fish and again he applauds with flippers. Then for the finish of the act there's a rack of horns and the seal goes in back of the rack and he blows into the horns and plays 'Yankee Doodle.' At the finish of 'Yankee Doodle' he presses on a lever, two American flags come up—you throw him a piece of fish. As he's applauding you're taking bows and the curtain comes down.

"I opened at the Dewey Theatre and got away with the act, but that night I had a date with a beautiful girl. Her name was Bertha Dufore. And she was also in show business. I was afraid to meet her. Because after you do four shows and your pockets are full of fish you don't smell good. And I met her and she never even noticed it because she was doing an act with Fink's Mules. In fact, she complimented me on my after-shave lotion.

"Well, anyways, I was a small-time vaudeville actor until I was twenty-seven years old, and then I got my big break and I married her. And even when I worked with Gracie I did nothing. We'd walk on the stage and I'd say to Gracie, 'How is your brother and she'd talk for seventeen minutes and I'd stand there smoking a cigar. Then at the finish of the act she did an Irish jig and I used to point to her feet. Then she would exit and I would follow her, and that's how I became a star. It wasn't easy. Sometimes I forgot to follow her.

"Well, that's the story of my life. In conclusion I want to thank the Friars for honoring me tonight and I want to thank you charming ladies and gentlemen for coming here tonight. And before I sit down I must tell you I've got a very, very, I thought of a very, very funny closing line. It's hilarious but I found out that Jack Benny thought of the same line. And as I've said, we've been friends for fifty-five years and to show you what a nice man I am, I'm going to let Jack do that line and I'm going to sit down without getting a laugh."

JACK BENNY closed the show:
"Thank you. Do you want to know something? This is the first time in my life that I ever felt it would be tough to follow George Burns. I never felt that way before. You know George and I have been friends for over fifty-five years and during the fifty-five years of our friendship we only had one argument and it could have been a very serious argument and could have led into a fight. But it only lasted half a minute. And I'll tell you what it was. A few months ago, when I was told that the Friars Club wanted to give George Burns a dinner, they wanted to give a dinner for us, I went to George Burns and I said, 'George, I will accept this testimonial dinner for us on one condition.' This is what started the argument. 'On one condition only. And it must be, your name must be first. All publicity must be George Burns and Jack Benny.' I say, 'Now don't argue with me, that's the only way I will accept this tribute. It's got to be George Burns and Jack Benny, your name first.' And

Jack Benny, Mary Livingstone, and Joan Benny in 1936 when he was still thirty-nine.

he said to me, 'Jack, I would prefer it the other way. I would prefer that your name be first.' So I said, 'all right,' and that ended the whole argument and we never fought again. That ended what could have been one of the biggest battles in show business.

"Everybody talked about Burt Reynolds and his posing in the nude. I was offered the same job of posing in the nude in one of those centerfold magazines. This happened to be true. It was not *Cosmopolitan.* Mine was *Popular Mechanics.* And they wanted a centerfold of me laying nude on my stomach on a lawn mower. For Christ sakes, I wouldn't take a chance like that for a million dollars. You know you can get hurt, you can get cut. I don't want to go through that again.

"I'm here to tell you that I love George Burns, that I think he's the funniest man in the world but he frustrates me by the fact that I can't make him laugh. Once I was playing in Minneapolis and I was living in a place called the Radison Hotel. And George Burns had to follow me in the next week, and he got into my hotel about eight o'clock in the morning of my closing day on a Saturday morning. And he called me from the lobby and he said, 'Jack, I'm in the lobby and I'll be right up to see you,' and I was tickled to death cause I love this guy no matter what he does to me.

"So I thought, 'What can I do to make this son of a bitch laugh when he comes into my bedroom?' Now this is true. So I took off my pajamas, it was eight o'clock in the morning, and I stood on top of the bed nude, absolutely nude. Now I wanted to look as silly as possible because he's tough to make laugh. So I took a book off the table, I put it on top of my head, and I held a glass of water in one hand and a rose in the other. Now that's the way I stood on top of the bed with a glass of water in one hand, a book on my head and a rose in the other hand.

"Now that is a pretty funny picture. You know, I mean it's not abstract but it's a funny picture. You would think that Burns would have to laugh. Well, he must have suspected something, because there I was, I swear, stark naked on top of the bed with a book on my head, a glass of water and a rose in my hands. There was a knock on the door, I said, 'Come in,' and he sent the maid in first. Now how do you explain to a maid that you're waiting for George Burns?

"Now this is something he did to me years ago. Let me tell you what he did to me about a year ago. He and I had to fly from Los Angeles to New York because the Friars were giving me a roast for television. George was one of the speakers and Vice-President Agnew was the host. So George and I flew in together and we took a suite of rooms at the Plaza—a big living room and two bedrooms, one on each end. I wanted to get a good night's sleep cause I wanted to be good on the show. About 3:30 or 4:00 in the morning, I feel someone tugging at my arm. And I'm sound asleep. And I wake up, can hardly see, and there is George standing there with a deck of cards in his hand. And he says to me, 'take a card.' Now I was so numb and so sleepy I didn't know what to do, so I took a card. I was a sort of pathetic figure, really in my sleep, I didn't know what I was doing, and I took a card. And he says to me, 'Look at it.' Now this is four o'clock in the morning. So I looked at the card and he said, 'Put it back in the deck.' So without knowing what the hell I was doing, I put the card back in the deck. He said, 'Thank you,' and went back to his own bed. I didn't sleep for the rest of the night. He slept fine.

"One time George and I decided that we would spend five days in Honolulu, a little vacation. We checked into a classy hotel. And I can remember this in detail exactly what happened cause I even remember the night cause you usually dress on Friday nights. So we got dressed and we were alone. And we go down and have dinner, we're dressed in black tie. And as we are eating dinner, a young fella walked over to me and introduced himself to me and I introduced him to George. And he said, 'Mr. Benny, you could do me a great favor.' I said, 'What is it?'

"He said, 'You can do me a great favor. I'm here with my grandmother. We also came from the mainland like you and Mr. Burns did. And my grandmother is celebrating, today she is celebrating her ninety-fifth birthday, ninety-five years old today, and she has followed your career ever since you were a little boy. She's followed you through your career in show business and vaudeville and pictures and radio and television, everything you've ever done, and she loves you so much that if you could meet her this would be the nicest birthday present that anybody ever received.' I said, 'I'd love to meet her' and I started to get up and he said, 'No, you sit here with Mr. Burns, finish your dinner, and when you're through I'll bring her over to meet you.'

"He walks away for about ten minutes and comes back with his grandmother, really ninety-five years old. She had the most beautiful face, white hair, and she was on a cane, but she was kind of hobbling over. And she had a quiver in her voice. You know sometimes I cry when I tell this story. I'm not kidding, I'm not kidding about this, she was so sweet. And he introduced me to his grandmother, this little old lady bent over on the table, and George is just sitting there looking at her. And in a quivering voice this old lady said to me, 'Mr. Benny,' this is holding on to her cane, she says, 'This is the most beautiful present, birthday present, I've ever received in my whole life. Just to think in all the years that I've known you and you've never known me and how much I've loved you.'

"And she kept telling me how many years she has loved me and loved me and adored me. And she just did all the talking while she was there at the table. And finally, after we talked for a long time, she started to leave, she said, 'May I kiss you?' I gave her a kiss and then she hobbled away with her grandson and as she got away George Burns turned to me and said, 'Well, looks like you're all set up for tonight.' And to show you what a dirty man he is, I cleaned up the finish. He didn't say it in just those words. I just cleaned it up.

"Would you like to hear one more? All right. One day Jerry Lewis, a mutual friend of ours, a comedian, came to me and he said, 'Jack, how would you like to get even with George Burns for all the dirty, lousy tricks he has played on you?' I said, 'I'd love to.' He said, 'He has a birthday coming up pretty soon,' which, of course, I knew about. He said, 'Why don't you on his birthday send him a beautiful necktie and have a note in it written by a lady saying, "I love you," and don't let her sign her name. Next day send him another beautiful necktie.' Now Jerry Lewis is the one who told me, 'Send him another beautiful necktie, have the same lady write on the card "I love you,' don't let her sign her name. And do this every day, and eventually it'll drive George crazy and then you being the closest friend, he will have to call you and tell you what his problem is. Then you will have the laugh on him.'

"So I did it. Every day I sent him a most beautiful necktie and I had my secretary, a lady, write "I love you" on it. I wouldn't let her sign her name. And the next day another necktie, and the next day another necktie, and the next day another one, and each time a card saying "I love you," no name. And sure enough, in three weeks (meanwhile it cost me a fortune in ties) and in about three weeks Mr. Burns here called me. He says, 'You can stop with the ties, I need shirts now.' So I said to him, 'George, for God sakes, how did you know it was me?' And he said, 'Who do you think told Jerry Lewis to tell you to send me the ties?'

"Anyway, this was a lovely evening and I do want to thank all the ladies and gentlemen here on the dais, this dignified dais, these wonderful people, including Mary Livingstone who never goes with me anyplace. She never travels with me anyplace. This is the first time in a long time. She lets me go away seven, eight weeks at a time, she trusts me, you know. It's kind of sad that she can, but then she does."

12

Mike Todd

There was no Friars Club dinner in honor of producer Mike Todd at the Waldorf-Astoria on Sunday night, March 23, 1958. Even though 1,200 people had paid fifty dollars a person the ballroom was dark. Even though $5,000 of the money raised was to be given to Mike Todd's personal charity, college scholarships for black children, the curtain was down. And even though Earl Wrightson was to sing "The Star Spangled Banner" and Jack E. Leonard was to MC and the dais was to be dressed with Lucille Ball, Gypsy Rose Lee, Alan King, Elsa Maxwell, Robert Merrill, Jack Barry, Polly Bergen, Dick Rodgers, former Attorney General Herbert Brownell, Oscar Hammerstein, Mayor Robert F. Wagner, Joey Bishop, Ray Bolger, Jack Carter, Bobby Clark, Myron Cohen, Xavier Cugat, Abbe Lane, John Daly, Eddie Fisher, Phil Foster, Buddy Hackett, Governor Averill Harriman, Harry Hershfield, Eric Johnston, Sir Laurence Olivier, Marguerite Piazza, Debbie Reynolds, Jackie Robinson, Ginger Rogers, Peter Ustinov, Earl Wilson, and Spyros Skouras, the star could not be present and there could be no understudy.

The guest of honor who in this one year had captured two 14-karat awards—Elizabeth Taylor as his wife plus the Oscar for *Around the World in 80 Days*—had been killed the night before. His last appearance was somewhere in the rain-soaked Zuni Mountains, south of Grants, in the northwest central area of New Mexico known as the Badlands. His luxurious private plane, a twin-engine Lockheed Lodestar christened "The Lucky Liz," plowed into the side of the mountain at a 45-degree angle and exploded. It was a dentist who identified the body.

Todd, forty-nine, one of the greatest showmen since Barnum, would have valued the dramatic qualities of his exit: the offstage audience, the empty ballroom, the swift plunge out of joviality into despair, the partially written biography to have been titled *The First Nine Lives of Mike Todd,* the end of a career at its dizzying height, the last telephone call to his wife just before takeoff at Burbank Airport, the beautiful widow, twenty-six, grief-stricken, tear-stained, near collapse. Mrs. Elizabeth Taylor Todd, who had missed accompanying him on this fatal air trip because of a virus, was in shock.

Accompanying our guest of honor had been his pilot, copilot, and biographer. When Mike crashed he had been en route to New York. The sole purpose of the flight? To accept his Showman of the Year award from the Friars. Over the last twenty-five years Friars have awarded such testimonials to Joe E. Lewis, 1950; Jack Benny, 1951; Bob Hope, 1953; George Jessel, 1954; Dean Martin and Jerry Lewis, 1955; Ed Sullivan, 1956; Perry Como, 1957; Steve Allen, 1959; Dinah Shore, 1960; Garry Moore, 1961; Milton Berle, 1963; Joey Bishop, 1964; Johnny Carson, 1965; Sammy Davis, Jr., 1966; Steve Lawrence and Eydie Gorme, 1967; Barbra Streisand, 1969; Tom Jones, 1970; Alan King, 1971; Carol Burnett, 1973; Don Rickles, 1974; Frank Sinatra, 1976. This 1958 dinner in honor of Mike Todd with some $80,000 to be raised for the Relief Fund was the club's only dud.

At the time someone said that this was the way Mike would have wanted to go—at the height of his career and emblazoned on the front pages.

Mike Todd, born in Minneapolis and raised in Chicago, was a street fighter. He once told pals he was born with a silver spoon and then added, "But I stole it!" As a kid he organized crap games and his take was ten cents a pot. Approximately forty years later he was still a promoter, only he had promoted himself into millions. His *80 Days* was then playing in about thirty-six U.S. cities and 44 countries. The supercolossal epic, which had cost $6½ million to produce, had so far brought home $33 million.

Success flirted with Michael Todd, the son of Rabbi Chaym Goldbogen of Chicago. It played yo-yo with his life. He was broke. He was rich. He was broke again. "I may be broke but I'll never be poor," he said. He was married to Joan Blondell. He was married to Elizabeth Taylor. He lived life on a runaway horse. He was up. He was down. There were times when all his assets were wrapped up in the Havana he smoked.

Then he was up again. He segued from con man to connoisseur.

Mike Todd with Louella Parsons just before his fatal plane crash on his way to the Friars dinner in his honor.

He bought Picassos for his home, jewels for his wife. He threw a little $250,000 party for 18,000 guests at Madison Square Garden. He treated money like confetti and treated his friends with the same freehanded, freewheeling manner. When he had it, everybody had it. He spent big. He lived big. He died big.

It was the morning before, the Saturday morning before the Sunday night dinner, that Carl Timin, the then executive director of the club, heard the news. As he related it, "A member called me and told me, 'Mike has crashed.' I was annoyed. I told him, 'Cut it out. I don't have time for gags.' Some gag."

The thousands of souvenir programs were placed under lock and key. They've become collectors' items. The contents, intended to provoke laughter, presented page after page of sad ironies. Tributes from Irving Berlin, Rodgers and Hammerstein, Harry Belafonte,

Joe E. Lewis who wrote: "To a swell fella . . ." Berle wrote, "Congratulations." Grossinger's took a full page to reprint a photo of Todd and Mike, Jr., which had run in its own newspaper sixteen years earlier. Part of the caption read, "Mr. Todd, who is currently very active on Broadway, states that he has some important plans for the future." Standard airlines ads suddenly looked like sick jokes.

Nobody knew what to do. Master of Ceremonies Jack E. Leonard looked over his planned ad-libs. He was going to have said, "When Mike saw a recession coming he bought out a chain of employment agencies." He was going to have said, "When Mike was in Moscow he wanted to buy Elizabeth a sputnik but she refused because it wouldn't fit her wrist" . . . and "Wherever you go in show business you see the words 'Todd-AO.' Only a few years ago wherever you went you saw the words 'Todd IOU' " . . . and "Mike just came back from Russia. They didn't want him there either."

Joe E. Lewis wrote in the souvenir program: "Mike will always be a rich man as long as his friends have money . . . In a comparatively short time he worked his way up from a newsboy to Elizabeth Taylor . . . When Mike was old enough to realize how poor his folks were, he did something about it—he left home . . . At the age of sixteen he joined a circus. In less than three months he owned it. This was accomplished with three dice . . . At the age of twenty-five he made his mark. It was detected on a deck of cards . . . He had great foresight. Ten years ago he predicted that this year would be 1958 . . . Mike was always a great salesman. He could sell an American postcard to a Frenchman or a cooling system to an Eskimo . . . In honor of Mike Todd, we, the Friars, are planting an Arab in his name in Tel Aviv. . . ."

The huge wall-sized poster was still up, the tables in the Grand Ballroom were still set, and the Friars sent out their announcement. It was brief: "Due to the sudden death of our beloved member, Mike Todd, the Friars testimonial dinner in his honor which was to take place at the Waldorf-Astoria is canceled."

Two days later the following letter was sent to the guests who never arrived: "With the cancellation of the testimonial dinner to our deceased member and guest of honor, Mike Todd, the Friars did what they believed was the right and proper thing.

"Within the next few days, our board of governors will take

action with regard to the tickets you have purchased, and/or such advertising space to which you have subscribed.

"Please bear with us."

Circumstances forced the Friars to revert to an ancient format. The club came up with a Friars Frolic. Without a star and minus a stand-in or backup, the old socko, boffo Frolic was the only sure-fire vintage gambit to trot out. Fat Jack Leonard, dialectician Lou Holtz, quizmaster Jack Barry, and I divided the toastmastering.

The Copacabana exported its headliners to the Waldorf ballroom that night—singer Johnny Mathis and comedian Joey Bishop. From the Old Romanian (which was a nightclub as well as the guy who owned it) came comedienne Jean Carroll. The Latin Quarter donated Sallie Blair. From her apartment on Park Avenue trundled the all-time great broad of the saloons, Sophie Tucker. Other grade A spots were pop singer Georgia Gibbs, song 'n' dance man Johnny Johnston, the hot dance team the Szonys, and some twenty-two-man chorus who schlepped in from somewhere.

There was a sketch devoted to a "This Is Your Life" takeoff on Aaron Chwatt (this being Red Buttons's maiden name) starring Buttons, Dagmar (all three of her), Greta Thyssen, the Danish pastry who was Miss Denmark somewhere along the line, pint-sized Jerry Bergen, and movie star Robert Alda. Pat Boone did something else. Double-talker Al Kelly did something else. Walter Cronkite and John Daly did some audience participation. Bob Hope addressed the assemblage, bidding them "have no fear because somewhere on some lonely frontier Elvis Presley is defending us" and a good night was had by all.

With this trip down the Yellow Brick Road, the Friars made the best of a Eugene O'Neill situation. There was some controversy about whether the souvenir journals printed for the original dinner should have been distributed. Eventually they were left on the chairs enclosed in their envelopes. It felt sort of symbolic. At least in this way it was an honest admission that Mike was there in spirit.

A thousand heads and bodies showed. The fete raised about $65,000. Even in absentia master showman Mike Todd proved he could still pull off a hell of a show.

13

The Friar

The first time I heard myself paged over the loudspeaker: "Friar Joey Adams, please answer the phone, *Friar Joey Adams*," I really got a kick out of it.

I was always welcome at the Friars. They were always polite and pleasant. I appeared on the dais for them at luncheons and dinners, I entertained at their parties, but I was always a guest. Now it was my club. I wasn't Mr. Adams or Joey anymore. I was Friar Joey Adams.

Until now I was always somebody's guest because no cash changes hands. Only a Friar can stand you to a meal. A member just signs for whatever he and his guests have. A guest can't even spring for the tip. Automatically 17 percent is added on the check and that's divided among the waiters, busboys, headwaiter, and probably even the assistant pastry chef for all I know.

Not even the checkroom attendant accepts gratuities. Try to slip Albert a few for being so pleasant and he points to a sign that says "No tipping permitted. Thank you." Same goes for the bartenders and the rest of the staff.

Becoming a member meant that now I was stuck with my own tabs, and I know you're not going to believe it, but I liked the idea. I actually enjoyed signing my tabs with the special number assigned to me. I felt like a big man. I was a Friar.

Milton Berle and Henny Youngman proposed me for membership, and it took a long while before I was accepted. At first I thought it was something personal. Jackie Green, an old friend and VP at I.C.M., the international theatrical agency, who is also chairman of the admissions committee, explained: "Everybody is treated the same. It's the rules. See, there are fifteen men on the board. They discuss each applicant and then one guy interviews you and then your name is posted on the bulletin board for six to eight weeks in case a member has a special beef against you and then your name is submitted to the entire membership."

"Good idea," I said, "in case somebody finds you were a Nazi or a Communist spy or you laid an egg in Buffalo or something."

All you need are two nays to be blackballed which, I guess, is better than the Lambs where it can be thumbs down with only one. Also you never know who didn't like you or who kept you out because the board of governors vote is strictly a secret ballot. I ruminated on the possibility that maybe somebody who saw my name on the bulletin board didn't like me because I borrowed his monologue or forgot to introduce him at a benefit or didn't put him on my radio show or maybe a member wrote in that we had a large inventory of comics in the Friars already. I only know that eight weeks after my name was submitted to the membership committee, I was getting embarrassed.

I was a little apprehensive, although I did have something on my side. Two-thirds of the membership must be in show business and that I was unless, maybe, they didn't think my act belonged in the business. Actually, I thought I had the right credentials for the two-thirds part. I had been president of the American Guild of Variety Artists for six years, I was goodwill ambassador for three presidents of the United States, I headed the Actors' Youth Fund, and represented Presidents Kennedy and Johnson in a cultural siege of Southeast Asia. Besides that, I had worked for Jackie Green in Asia and had been on the bill many times with Dean Buddy Howe when he was Carroll and Howe in vaudeville. I had paid my check for admission to Walter Goldstein. What was the delay? Why hadn't they called me?

Is it possible two finks had blackballed me?

It had happened to Milton Berle. He had the distinction of being kayoed at the Friars *and* the Lambs. In 1950 he decided he wanted to become a member of the Lambs Club. "I knew a lot of the members," he told me. "I had been taken to their clubhouse for several great evenings. I had entertained at their benefits. They seemed to want me and I wanted them. So I was put up for membership. There were some great Lambs behind me: William Gaxton, Jack Waldron, even Bert Lytell, the shepherd of the club. To everybody's surprise, especially mine, I was blackballed."

It takes only one blackball, and the one who drops it in doesn't have to identify himself. "I was depressed when it happened"

Milton told me later. "I know there are always people who don't like you. I guess that's part of making it in show business. But you don't think about it, surely not this way. Suddenly it was right out in the open. Except that it wasn't in the open because I didn't know who did it. At first I thought it was Frank Fay who never liked me or my kind, but I wasn't sure.

"Once a year I was put up for membership and each time I was blackballed. I was also blackballed after Frank Fay died and finally the story came out. It was Bert Lahr who had been knifing me all along. It seems he felt I was doing his material or imitating him or upstaging him or something. The truth is, I was a fan of his. I thought he was a great comedian. I even put him in my shows, but he was a closet hater and now his hate was showing.

"When the Lambs called on him in 1956 and told him they wanted me in the club, he was still bitter and threatened, 'If you take Berle—I'll resign.' 'We'll accept your resignation,' they said."

Berle was blackballed by the Friars as far back as 1939. Whereas it took only two to knock you out of the box, he had three. He knew who the guys were, too, because they bragged about it. The cast of characters featured Frank Fay, Harry Jans of Jans and Whalen, and Buster West of Wells, Virginia and West, vaudevillians all.

When Milton tried to trace their hates he found that Frank Fay was bitter because Berle was funny and with *his* material, he said. Buster West had some other itch—about a girl or billing or something. Vaudevillians Jans and Whalen were angry from a different picture altogether. They didn't want any more of "those kind" of comedians around.

Berle's hurt lasted five years. He didn't submit to membership until 1944, and only eight months later he became the abbot. Some say it was Milton Berle who saved the club.

"I couldn't understand it," Milton mused when we discussed it recently. "I've always loved the Friars. As far back as 1921 when it was Elizabeth Kennedy and Milton Berle, we did the Friars Frolic at the Metropolitan Opera House. I did shows with George M. Cohan, Enrico Caruso, Oscar Hammerstein, as well as Jans and Whalen, Frank Fay, and Buster West for the Friars. I could never understand that whole thing."

Berle was consistently in some kind of controversy. In his formidable years he was always in a feud with somebody—even if it was

140

Buddy Rogers and Mary Pickford at a Friars party in California.

one-sided. Another of his little capers was with producer Billy Rose
who quit the Friars in 1951 because of Milton.

Of course, Billy, who was a bigger than life showman, was not
always admired in terms of his character. For instance, he had
been married to the greatest comedienne of her day, Fanny Brice.
Billy had written dozens of hit songs such as "Barney Google,"
and produced dozens of hit shows such as *Jumbo*, and he owned
theatres and he owned nightclubs and he had millions. But his
ego was never satisfied. He couldn't take being billed as "Fanny
Brice's husband."

He decided to do something about it. At Times Square he put
up a tremendous electric sign that cost him a fortune. It read
simply, "Billy Rose." Twenty-four hours, night and day, it kept

flashing on and off "Billy Rose," "Billy Rose," "Billy Rose." Every dinnertime Rose stood there for an hour watching the sign holler out his name, "Billy Rose"—"Billy Rose"—"Billy Rose." One evening as he stood there admiring himself flashing up there in lights, he heard two Marines talking. One said, "Who the hell is Billy Rose?" And the other replied, "Fanny Brice's husband."

Somehow Milton became the target of people with problems. Billy Rose, as mighty a hater as he was a showman, was not the type to play second to anybody, and yet he was forced into that role with Milton. Milton had been married twice to the gorgeous blonde showgirl, Joyce Matthews. After their second divorce in 1948, it was Billy's turn to play the same scene and he played it line for line. He, too, married Joyce Matthews twice. Billy who was five foot four but had an ego that was six foot nine had an additional cross to bear. He was a member of a club that had Milton Berle as its abbot. To see his rival—who was not only taller than he but had gotten there first—taking bows all over *his* club was too much for Billy, so he quit.

Milton Berle's biggest problem was the other comedians. They all claimed he stole their material. The fact that he did it better had nothing to do with it. Milton admits he loved them all: "Bob Hope was really great," he says, "every time I went to see him, I laughed so hard I dropped my pencil." In fact, Milton later billed himself as "The Thief of Bad Gags."

Frank Fay, Jackie Osterman, Ricky Craig, Jr., and the other stand-up comics used to sit up nights at the Friars, Lambs, and Lindy's thinking how to get rid of this new fresh little Bronx kid who was stealing their jokes.

One Sunday night in December 1933, Bob Hope, who was in *Roberta* at the time, Jackie Osterman, and Ricky Craig, Jr., decided to teach Mighty Mouth a lesson. They found out where he was doing his benefits that night—five in all—they would go to all of them, ahead of Berle, and do all his routines and jokes. They went to the first three and murdered the people. Not only did they do all of Berle's jokes, they warned the audience not to tip Milton —let him die by himself.

Of course, Superlip laid such a series of omelets like the world has never known. Even his mother, who had started the laughs from the audience since he was five years old, couldn't get them going. "What's wrong with you, Milton?" she asked, as they went to each succeeding benefit. Milton had no answer.

Finally, Izzy Grove, the old champ, got to Milton and told him what was happening. Now Milton switched his timing and went to the Waldorf before the time he was scheduled, and did his act as well as all the Osterman, Craig, and Hope jokes—and he knew them all—including their parodies—*before* they arrived.

Then he stood quietly in the wings and watched them die. When they were ready to close the lid, Berle walked onstage. When Hope, Osterman, and Craig saw him they started to attack from all sides, but Milton just nodded to the orchestra leader who went into "The Star Spangled Banner." The audience stood up, of course, and the show was over.

Prior knowledge of these stories is sufficient for anybody to have qualms about being accepted in a club of his peers. The way I figured it, to be denied admission could really murder your ego. Particularly in a club of brotherhood . . . *Prae omnia fraternitas*, right?

It sure felt good to hear "Friar Joey Adams" coming over the loudspeaker. It meant there were no blackballs. I was a Friar. *Prae omnia fraternitas*. I answered the phone. It was Jackie Green, the head of the admissions committee, welcoming me to the club and reminding me to be at the cocktail party for new members: "Dean Buddy Howe is coming especially to give you a welcome hand."

I must tell you it was a special day for me. I walked under the white canopy into the clubhouse. Erne, Walter Goldstein's wife, was at the switchboard. She smiled and just pressed the button that opened the door for me to enter. It was a kick when Erne greeted me as "Friar Adams." It figured now that all the girls, Antoinette and Joan, would do the same. No asking who I was meeting anymore. It was my club and it was open sesame for me as I arrived.

Albert gave me a big smile and a pleasant greeting as he took my hat and coat. No check. He knows a good Friar when he sees one. I turned left into the little bar for a greeting drink with Joe the bartender who refused to give me a tab. It was an introductory drink to a new Friar.

The party for the new members was in the Milton Berle room opposite the Joe E. Lewis room, one flight up. I wanted the regal pleasure of walking up the handsome spiraled stairway instead of taking the elevator.

After the Chinese bartender, Gene, handed me my second opening drink, I asked Buddy Howe about the titles: "What does abbot mean? And how come you're the dean? You never went to college in your life. And why is William B. Williams called prior? And Robert Merrill is a monk?"

Buddy explained: "These are monastic titles. Sinatra is the abbot, or president; I am the dean, which means first vice-president; William B. is the prior, which is like second vice-president; Dr. Meylackson is the treasurer and that's the same in a monastery or a brothel; Red Buttons is the scribe, which is secretary.

"The rest are not elected. They are appointed by the board of governors. Sammy Davis Jr., is the bard; Johnny Carson is the knight; George Burns, proctor; Paul Anka, herald; Alan King, monitor; Alan Gale, historian; Robert Merrill, monk; George Hoffman, samaritan."

Prior William B. Williams said proudly, "This building was owned by Columbia University and during the Second World War part of the atom bomb was created here. They sold it to us because they knew we would not change the building proper, although we did have to promise them we would try not to lay any bombs here—on or off stage.

"It cost $325,000 in 1956 when the membership was a paltry 230. Today we boast 1,040, the figure that the board of governors decided would not be exceeded. To help the purchase of the building, a bond issue was raised of $100,000 from the membership only. This was paid off within three years and shortly thereafter the mortgage was paid off in full. All that besides more than a half million spent on refurbishing so that you now enjoy it all free and clear."

And I was going to enjoy it even if it wasn't exactly free. I walked up the carpeted spiral stairs with the heavy wooden banister like it was my own private mansion. Just like I've seen in the movies in all those millionaires' homes. On the third floor I saw Jesse Block tacking up a notice on the foyer bulletin board in front of the TV room and cardrooms. The notice said:

Nobody Is Perfect

Each one of us is a mixture of good qualities and some perhaps not-so-good qualities. In considering our fellow man we should remember his good qualities and realize that his faults only prove that he is, after all, a human being. We should refrain from making harsh judgment of a person just because he happens to be a dirty, rotten, no-good son of a bitch!

144

Friar Phil Silvers was lolling in the TV room watching himself in some one-reeler he had filmed during the Revolutionary War. The Friars had laid out $5,000 for cable TV because it was important that the actors get a chance to watch themselves on the screen and to show off to the producers and agents and managers who were members. Cable TV is usually a staple of big buildings and is amortized by all the tenants paying a piece of it, but when you're only one tenant you have to pay the whole thing. It was worth it, though, just to watch Phil Silvers enjoying himself—and to get him away from the card table for a few minutes.

I stepped into the cardroom and waved at Irving Caesar, Goody Ace, Killer Joe Piro, and Jule Styne, who were in the midst of a hot pinochle game or klabiash or poker or something. I only know I coughed, said hello, burbled good-bye, offered greetings, but it was like I was painted on the wall. Or it was like they were all losing. Nobody answered me. Nobody even looked up. I backed out like I had stepped into a CIA meeting by mistake.

On the fourth floor, writer Eli Basse was all alone in the billiard room practicing in case he ran into a pool shark or a sucker. I'm not exactly a pool fan but I spent an hour there just looking at the pictures on the walls of all the past and present Friars who had made history in show business.

I dropped by the office next to the poolroom and paid my dues, made an appointment with Mike the barber and Shoshana the Israeli manicurist and hoisted myself up to the fifth floor for a steam and massage. Milton Berle and Jan Murray were on their way in. "Tom Jones, William B., Paul Anka, and Stanley Adams, the head of ASCAP, are in there," the masseur, David Leon, told us, "so if you want a massage, you better make an appointment now."

"How much is a massage" I asked, "I'm a new member."

"Three dollars," he said, "for old or new members—big or small bodies alike."

"Compared to Broadway that's pretty cheap," Jan said. "Of course, the rubbers in the massage parlors there are built different and rub different things."

Milton said, "I know, I've been to one of them. They ran out of rubbing alcohol for three days and nobody noticed."

A square from the one-third segment of the membership known as "civilians" approached Milton and said: "They tell me you're supposed to be the greatest endowed of all the show people. Personally I always thought that's a joke. I think I am bigger than you even if I'm not in show business."

"Well," Jan grinned, "we're all going into the steam room and we'll soon find out if 'all men are created equal' like Lincoln said."

The square insisted, "How about a little bet, before we go inside. I bet 100 bucks I'm better endowed than Berle. We'll let Joey Adams be the judge."

In the steam room we recognized Stanley Adams through the fog. He was getting ready for the big ASCAP night in the Monastery downstairs. All the songwriters would be there to honor Stanley: Sammy Cahn of "Three Coins in the Fountain," Mitchell Parish with his "Star Dust," Benny Davis of "Margie" immortality, and Lou Alter "Manhattan Serenade," Gerald Marks "All of Me," and Yip Harburg and Eubie Blake and Jule Styne.

"Congratulations," Jan said, "it should be a great night. You deserve it. All the songs you've written and what you've done for the songwriters and . . ."

"Let's face it," Milton said to Stanley, "you're our guest of honor only because our cardroom has a deficit of $3,000 and you'll help us raise the money."

Stanley replied, "Milton, I've seen you work in a lot of places, but this is the first time I ever saw you MC a steam room."

"Hey, Milton," Jan hissed, peering off into the steam. "I just saw Tom Jones. I think you lost the title."

Gene Baylos was waiting for me on the second floor. We were going to break a little boiled beef together in the Joe E. Lewis room. "No disrespect," I said to Uncle Miltie, "but I had cocktails in *your* room a little while ago."

"Good," Milton boomed, "in that case we're all your guests for dinner. If it was in the Milton Berle room, I would have picked up the tab."

"I'm sure I could switch rooms. I . . ."

"I wouldn't think of it," Milton said, banging me on the back. "Anyway, you're a new Friar and you should pick up a check for a change. Your money talks with a stutter. You got a physical handicap. You're hard of spending."

"I'm meeting Baylos," I said, "I owe him a dinner."

"Now," Milton zinged, "there's a spender. If he was at the Last Supper he would have asked for separate checks."

I was the best man when Gene Baylos got married October 24,

146

1954. At least, I outbid everybody for the job. I promised to pay for the music, the flowers, and the rabbi as well as a dinner every year for the bride and groom. This was the twentieth anniversary for Gene and Cyril and, of course, I was the underwriter.

I remember the wedding so well. I had arranged for Rabbi Burstein of the Actors' Temple to officiate. When Gene saw him he instructed, "Look Rabbi, don't do more than eight minutes, you'll lose the crowd." The hip rabbi said, "Look, Mr. Baylos, I gave up a very important funeral to perform this ceremony, so don't bug me."

Gene Baylos is a comedian's comedian. "That means," Berle snarled, "only about eight people like him." Since I was picking up the tab I insisted that Gene earn his board and tell us one of the famous Baylos stories.

"I was working at Charlie's in Little Ferry, New Jersey," Gene told us. "Fifty a week and 10 percent to the agent. The boss, a real tough character, I think his name was Funge or Nuncio or something, called me over after the first show. I wasn't exactly a hit but what can you expect for 50 less 10 percent. 'Hey, comic,' he said, 'what are you? Where you from?'

" 'I'm a Hungarian Jew,' I told him.

" 'Hey, I like that stuffed cabbage. You got that?'

" 'Sure,' I said. 'I'll have my mother make some for you.'

"Every night I brought him my mother's stuffed cabbage. For twenty weeks I was held over. My act wasn't too good but my mother's stuffed cabbage was a big hit. One night my mother ad-libbed and sent him some stuffed peppers. The next night I was fired: 'That stuffed pepper gave me heartburn. I didn't sleep all night. You're troo. Screw. Pick up your pots and get the hell out of here.' "

"I saw your act," Jan Murray piped up, "I hope your wife makes good stuffed cabbage."

"That's my trouble," sighed Gene, "I'm too good to everybody and they don't appreciate it. Only last night I saw a bum in the street in front of the clubhouse. He was so cold he was blue, and no coat or hat. I told him to walk home with me and I'd get him a coat. I ran upstairs and got him one of my best coats and put it on him. The color came back in his face as he wrapped it around him. He put it to the light and said, 'Hey, Mister, what color is this?' I said it was brown. 'Brown?' he hollered, 'brown? I can't wear brown —it does nothing for me—I hate brown.' "

14

Harry Hershfield

The most delicious evening I ever spent at the club was in the company of my theatrical godfather on his eighty-eighth birthday. Harry Hershfield had shown me how to take my first show-business steps. He had shown me how to do my first gags. Not only that but he had given me my first gags to do.

Harry went from $2.50 a week in 1899, when he worked for the Chicago *Daily News,* to cartoonist (Desperate Desmond, Abe Kabibble) to vaudeville in 1912 with Eddie Cantor and George Jessel. In the forties he emerged as a storyteller-cum-laude when he was the star of radio's longtime program "Can You Top This," and at this point, in his twilight years, he was still the greatest afterdinner speaker in America.

Aldo Spagnoli, the very pleasant maître d', escorted us into the red plush dining room with its wood paneling and its paintings of the all-time big-timers and seated us under the portrait of Al Jolson. Harry requested the "Program," and with a flourish Aldo handed him the menu. Everybody talks show biz there. "Let's get the show on the road," chef Ben Gomez, who has been with the club over twenty-five years, said to his assistant Angelo Rodriguez when they heard Harry was there.

Harry could eat only special foods and as they brought him the chicken in the pot which he dearly loved, he reached into his pocket and brought out a yellowed page. It was a poem from a century-old Friars program. It had been written by Sam M. Lewis who authored "Rockabye" and many of Jolie's biggest hits. It was entitled "Memories" and was signed S.M.L.

"MEMORIES"

by S. M. L.

Listen my children and you shall hear
The Tale of the Friars of Yesteryear

Their home was built with laughter and song
  Where squabbles and hatred, did not belong
The walls seem'd to echo—with good cheer
  whenever an actor would appear

Breaking a jump—from God knows where
  A Sunday open—an extra fare
But a Trouper couldn't resist the "Bang"
  To say Hello—to his old gang

And here are the names you'd meet each day
  One block east, from old Broadway
Will Rogers—Hitchcock and Georgie Cohan
  Sam Bernard and Louis Mann

Al Jolson—Dockstader—Montgomery and Stone
  Victor Herbert—Gershwin and Baldy Sloan
the Mortons—James Norton and Eddie Foy
  And Willie Collier, the laughing boy

James J. Corbett, Old Gentleman Jim
  Walter C. Kelly—remember him?
Jimmy Walker and Wilton Lackaye
  Each one a star—in the starry sky

If I omitted a single one
  Who made this world—a world of fun
I'm really sorry—But my pen I think
  Is wet with tears—instead of ink

The bows we take—with so much fuss
  Really doesn't belong to us
They were the "Cloak"—We're just the "Hem"
  And all the credit belongs to them

They built your home—they kept it warm
  A home that weathered ev'ry storm
Strong of steel and mellowed wood
  But the cornerstone was brotherhood

Sing—Here's to the Friars—Here in the hall
  And to those that have answered the last curtain call
To them we are thankful for many things
  But mostly for "prompting us" from the wings.

"The wonderful thing about living in the past," Harry commented, "is that you cannot be dispossessed. Y'know, I loved that poem. I knew all those guys he talks about. Don't forget I was secretary of the Friars when George M. was abbot."

Harry was clearly in the mood to reminisce. He told me about

George M. whom he said had as great a respect for his parents as he did for show business. "Once George and I were talking about the new dirty shows that were making a lot of money. I asked him how much he lost by not staging that kind of stuff. He said, 'I'd rather get cleaned by clean shows than have my father take me over his knee for putting something on that would make my mother and him ashamed.'

"One time a rich slob went to Cohan and asked him to put a certain chippy in the chorus of a forthcoming Cohan and Harris production. George asked the girl's sponsor three quick questions: 'Is she willing to work as hard as I do and a little bit harder? Can she sleep without first being rocked in a limousine? Can I take her home to have dinner with my father and mother and wife and children?'

"Maybe I wouldn't believe the story myself if I wasn't there to hear it—and watch the patron of the potential chorus girl withdraw his application."

"Were they really such great days?" I asked Harry.

"These are better," he answered. "Y'know, when you get to be my age everybody old becomes religious. We say, 'Gosh, that old teacher was great'; even if she was an old bag. Every gray-haired witch becomes Whistler's Mother.

"Guys like George Jessel and George Burns are at the age where they cry at card tricks. When I look back I only look back at the fun things. Like the time Archbishop Fulton J. Sheen consented to appear on his friend Jackie Gleason's TV show. During rehearsals the archbishop suddenly found himself in the midst of organized confusion with electricians, directors, musicians and, of course, a gross of scantily dressed chorus girls.

"Jackie was rushing around as usual, but he stopped for a second when he saw his distinguished guest star. 'Say, your excellency,' he winked, 'did I see you looking at my chorus girls?'

" 'Yes, you did,' Sheen smiled.

" 'Ah-ah,' Jackie said, teasing, 'isn't that a no-no?'

"His grace merely shrugged, 'Just because I'm on a perpetual diet it doesn't mean I can't study the menu once in a while.' "

"You've known them all," I said to Harry. "Were the old stars—the old pros—any different than the ones around today?"

"Actors are always the same," he answered. "They are the originators of the credo of blood, sweat, and tears. They give blood to the Red Cross; they sweat to make the big time; they shed tears when one performance out of a thousand dies. A ham can be led and bled, used and abused, kicked and caressed, and he always comes up smiling—if anybody's watching.

"I'll tell you the greatest show-business story of all. The first film made by Alfred Lunt and Lynn Fontanne titled *The Guardsman* was good, but they, perfectionists that they are, were unsatisfied. Miss Fontanne was first to view the film's rushes and she sped back to their suite where her husband was waiting and burst into tears.

" 'Alfred, Alfred!' she cried. 'We're ruined! I've seen the rushes. You photograph without lips and I come out old and haggard and ugly. My tongue is thick and I lisp, and I walk like a walrus. I have lines in my face. My feet are too big, and my clothes look like a sack. I'm a mess with my stringy hair and deformed body.' Just then her tears overcame her voice and she faltered. In the silence that ensued Lunt muttered, 'No lips, eh?' "

"I wish I could have been around in those days," I said. "I wish I could have been at the Friars Frolic of 1933 at the New Amsterdam Theatre when MC Friar Lou Holtz introduced Friar Governor Alfred E. Smith who did a song and dance routine that stopped the show cold. What was it like to be a Friar in those days?"

Harry has spoken at every important dinner since the Last Supper. He knew them all. And he reminisced for me: "In over a half-century the Friars have more than witnessed the passing scene of the metropolis. Let me give you a montage of those days: Caruso, with adoring society women falling at his feet, enjoyed standing in front of the Knickerbocker Hotel making mental 'passes' at passing shopgirls. 'Trick Waiter' Luke Barnett making unsuspecting Lillian Russell blush and cry at a banquet when Luke said loudly to her, 'What kind of bringing up have you had—you are eating with the wrong fork!'

"While Broadway and 42nd Street was the northern border of George M. Cohan's 'Homesick' songs, below 39th Street was the Tenderloin of Manhattan. Eighth Avenue and this Broadway didn't invent the street of prostitutes. In these days I witnessed fifty or more streetwalkers at one time circling the Met Opera House after closing, plying their trade. The infamous Haymarket on Sixth Avenue was certainly the place to meet the elite of New York.

"The Café d'Opera was very posh but it lasted merely a few months for it only allowed those in who wore white tie and tails. When the headwaiter was the only one dressed that way the high-class jernt folded.

"Past the Metropole, now Rosoff's restaurant, is where I used to stroll. I was around when Rosenthal was gunned by Police Lieutenant Becker's gangsters during a vice-scandal investigation. I heard the shots but found myself like the fellow who described a shooting: 'I heard the bullets twice. Once when it passed me and once when I passed it.'

"In those days murder, rape, and robbery was more of a retail business than the wholesale trade it is today. I attended every opening of Ziegfeld's *Follies,* by the way. Lillian Lorraine, trapeze-swinging over the audience—her buttocks reflected on the bald heads below—was the hope of producer Ziegfeld who was always looking for amour in all its manifestations. Incidentally, Ziegfeld spoke with a lisp and not in stentorian voice as he has been pictured in films.

"Traffic conditions were as bad in those horse and carriage days as they are today. Took me over an hour to get from 59th and Broadway to 42nd Street in a hansom. Today's gasoline odor is nothing compared to the geshtank of hundreds of horses in sweat on a warm night. The date with you knew what to blame and took it with a laugh. Carriage wheels caught in all sorts of things caused delays and much profanity. If you think those were the 'good old days,' you're lying to yourself.

"The many fight clubs where a wallet in your back pocket wasn't there long because the filchers could walk under the benches and pick at ease. At the old Madison Square Garden the overcoat that you were sitting on was pulled out from under you as you jumped up to cheer the six-day bike riders.

"I remember Caruso on his way to a Met performance singing to a group of his countrymen down in a hole they were digging in the middle of the street. I remember Lorber's memorable restaurant across the Met where Caruso gourmandized to his untimely fate. I remember musical shows that had at least six numbers that were hit tunes instead of the one or two today that make more money recording than did all the stars combined in those unrecording days.

"And I remember the unbelievable and hectic actors' strike with Louis Mann on the rear of a truck yelling about the help for the cause and saying: 'I hold in my hand an anonymous check for $5,000!' George M. Cohan representing the managers fighting the actors made a public vow: 'I will run an elevator before I'll give in to the performers. . . .' In that melee I witnessed a stagehand beating up a sanctimonious David Belasco and saying to the famous producer: 'Your phony clerical collar doesn't mean a thing to me!'

"I've heard a lot of stories about the great wit of some of the old-timers," I said, "were they really great wits? I mean guys like Walter Kelly, Louis Mann, Will Rogers—were they as funny as Hope or Berle or me, for instance?"

"Well," Harry said, "nobody could have been as funny as you—I mean the way you dress—but the others were witty in terms of the native wit. It's tough to compare because everything has changed. You see, in 1916 the board of governors of the Friars raised their initiation fee to $60 and all lay members $100. Today it's $600 and $1,000. Well, it's that way with wit. The standards have been raised.

"These stories happened in 1916. Friar Billy Jerome, the celebrated songwriter of 'Bedelia' and many other smash songs, was sent a telegram by a singer, which said 'Billy Jerome, Strand Building, New York City. Send me song. If good, will send check.' Jerome replied: 'Send me check—if good will send song.'

"Friar Walter Kelly, known the world over as the Virginia Judge, was noted for his ready wit. He was accosted by a fellow Friar who asked him if he was going to Florida for the winter. Without hesitation he answered, 'I don't know. My wife hasn't made up my mind yet.'

"Friar Louis Mann had a fondness for peculiar shaped collars and walking into a Fifth Avenue haberdashery he was shown some of his favorite kinds by the obliging clerk. When asked the price the clerk answered, 'Two for twenty-five cents.' 'How much for this one?' Mann asked. 'Fifteen cents' was the reply. 'All right,' said Mann, 'I'll take the other one.'

"Where else but in the Friars could a kibitzer, Rube Bernstein, tear up a deck of cards because his kibitzee wasn't winning?"

We were sitting opposite a portrait of Will Rogers, which reminded Harry of a story. Everything reminded Harry of a story: "At a roast for the movie czar Will Hays the principal speaker was Will Rogers. Will drawled: 'I brought to this hotel here tonight a 15- or 20-minute speech—15 without laughs, 20 with laughs. As I came in, a gentleman says to me, 'I see you're going to give us some stuff on Hays.' Well sir, you could have knocked me over with a feather. After they told me to talk about the biggest amusement business in the world, I went home and prepared this address on bootlegging.'"

15

A Star Is Born

America's greatest songs and some "big, big shews" and many a headliner were born in the Friars clubrooms. Ed Sullivan plucked several future comers out of our special talent nights as have some of the biggest agents in the low-priced field.

Freddie Prinze was reluctantly discovered at one "New Talent Night." When Dave Jonas offered to present his new Puerto Rican find, Walter Goldstein rejected him: "I hear this kid is okay but he's too dirty. This isn't a stag, you know."

"Look," Jonas said, "if he gets dirty, I'll scrub him down myself. Now will you listen to me and put him on? He'll break up the joint. Will you take my word for it?"

His word was pretty good. The kid was not only a sensation but right after that Jonas signed him for "Chico and the Man."

Now a roving talent scout for his own agency, Dave has presented such fine new comedians at the "Nights at the Friars" as Billie Baxter, Dick Capri, Dick Lord, Vic Arnell, and Freddie Roman who himself is now chaperoning other young comics to their place in the sun.

There have been special nights for Billy Eckstein, Joe Franklin, Dave Brubeck, Lionel Hampton, the Barry Sisters, Enzo Stuarti, Steve and Edie, and often some cockamamie unknown hits big.

You can never tell who will dress the audience those nights. Earl Wilson could show up and do a story about you or Buddy Howe and Jackie Green could push you as extra-added attraction with one of their Italian boy singers or a producer or director or writer could spot you for a TV series or a Broadway show or at the very least a Saturday night in the Catskills.

"I guess because I was a civilian in a show-business world, I had the chutzpah to start those special nights," Walter Goldstein told me. "But when some agent brought Bette Midler to me one night and asked to put her on I said, 'Forget it—she looks like a schreck.' Her hair was a mess—her clothes were early Salvation Army—and furthermore the agent who brought her wasn't known to me.

"Anyway, one of the stars didn't show and I put her on in desperation. All I can tell you is that by my own ignorance a star was born. They cheered this unknown girl like my other 'discovery' Freddie Prinze. She got the longest standing ovation I ever saw at the club, which proves what I know about show business."

What happened to Bette and Freddie since I don't know. But I do know that Walter will never again refuse any new act brought to him by an agent—especially if it's Dave Jonas that does the bringing.

After that, the club started a Friarling drive to bring in members under twenty-six. A Friarling pays little dues for a couple of years until he makes it. At this first swearing-in ceremony, Abbot Emeritus Milton Berle spotted a Friarling who was completely bald. "When it comes to age," Milton cracked, "I think Jack Benny does his counting."

A gaggle of young comedians joined up to push their careers along on those special nights. This triggered the older funny men who joined to be born all over again. Any one of those nights you can find a Jimmy Joyce, Joey Villa, Morty Storm, Sandy Baron, Charlie Callas, Joe Maury, Larry Best, Rodney Dangerfield, Pat Cooper, Pat Henry, Gene Baylos, or even me.

The Monastery has always been a grade A audition hall. One night in the fall of 1931 the "Saturday Night Boys" were laying on a party for Friar Bing Crosby who was shoving off for Hollywood. Paramount Pictures had signed him for his first shot. He was one of the stars of a musical production.

It was a particularly funny night, but the hit of the night were two little known pop composers who were introduced by Toastmaster Jack Benny. Friars Mack Gordon and Harry Revel were a smash playing and singing their own songs. Walter Winchell, one of the speakers on the dais, introduced himself and asked, "Where have you boys been hiding?" The boys were too stunned to reply. Winchell continued, "Well, guys, I'm taking you out of your hiding place." He did just that in his columns. Barely six bars later that publicity paid off and they were signed by Paramount to write scores for musical pictures.

Their first assignment was *Sitting Pretty*, which boasted the smash song hit "Did You Ever See a Dream Walking?" They followed that with *We're Not Dressing,* which united them with their old Friar chum Crosby and included Ethel Merman, Burns and Allen, and a juvenile who had a walk-on—Ray Milland. It was in this flick that Crosby scored with two great songs, "Love Thy Neighbor" and "Stay as Sweet as You Are." And that's the once-upon-a-time saga of Gordon and Revel who went forth from the Friars to find fame and fortune.

And about that young groaner the Friars shipped Westward Ho in 1931—before he ever laid eyes on his first orange he'd worked dates like the Mosque Theatre in Newark, New Jersey, for two weeks for $150 so he hasn't done too badly either.

Let me tell you about one particular song that was born at the Friars. It was about 1:30 A.M., the year was 1917. Cluttering up the Round Table were such folks as Will Rogers, artist Harrison Fisher, Willie Collier, not a bad comedian, Abbot George M. Cohan, and "Gentleman Jim" Corbett. The central figure, though, was Richard Harding Davis, the renowned war correspondent who had just returned from the front.

Naturally, the conversation centered around the war. They were debating the U.S. strategy vociferously. Everyone was trying to get Dick Davis's firsthand opinions, but he refused to be drawn in. Two rounds of drinks later the controversy had reached battle proportions.

Amidst the bombs bursting in air George M. hauled his musical director, Charley Gebest, to the piano. After fifteen or twenty minutes of noodling, Cohan turned and addressed his pals, asking if they would care to hear a little tune he had just thought of. It was built around a bugle call, he said.

Pandemonium broke loose. The boys joined in and wouldn't stop singing. They loved it. For those in the Friars Monastery that early morn a classic was born. Soon bands were playing it, soldiers and sailors were marching to it, and all the free world was singing it:

> Over there, over there—send the word, send the word
> Over there, that the Yanks are coming, the Yanks are coming
> The drums rum-tumming every where.
> So prepare, say a prayer, send the word,
>   send the word to beware
> We'll be over, we're coming over,
> And we won't be back till it's over over there.

Many stanzas later, Henry Watterson, a music publisher, and composer George Meyer were lunching at the club. Watterson, who also owned a racing stable, invited George to watch one of his thoroughbreds compete.

Meyer accepted and snuggled luxuriously into the soft and roomy splendor of the custom car. He marveled at the good taste that the wealthy publisher displayed in his choice of wheels. In fact, this glorious limo was only one in a collection of half a dozen. While purring along, Meyer asked Mr. Watterson, "How about a tip on one of your horses?"

"Why?"

"Because I want to win enough money to get a car like this!"

"What do you want a car for?"

"I want it for me and my gal."

Watterson made this proposal: "You deliver me a hit song and I'll give you an automobile."

Meyer took the publisher at his word. Getting together with Edgar Leslie and E. Ray Goetz, Meyer's purpose became the title of his song, "For Me and My Gal."

Oh, yes, George Meyer got the car—and lost it on Watterson's next tip.

The Friars Frolic of 1911 was to be the first road Frolic attempted by the club (fourteen cities in fourteen days) and the entire project was under the direction of Abbot George M. Cohan. Musty old Bryant Hall, the rehearsal area for most of the early nineteen hundred shows, was like a try-on for a revolution as singers, dancers, jugglers, acrobats, and minstrels ran around doing their bits or limbering up waiting to be called.

Squashed into this array of creative talent was a rising, young twenty-three-year-old tunesmith. The program scheduled Irving Berlin to render his popular song, "My Wife's Gone to the Country."

Unobtrusive and standing by himself near the door of the main rehearsal hall, the modest young composer was quietly awaiting the summons to come forward and play his number. Behind him the door opened and Freddie Block entered. The Frolic's company manager, Block was also the director of the theatrical ventures of heavyweight champions James J. Corbett and Bob Fitzsimmons.

"What are you waiting for, Irving?" he asked.

"I'm waiting for Mr. Cohan to call me."

Jokingly, the ebullient little manager asked, "You mean to tell me the writer of today's most famous song hit has to stand in the rear of the room and await a summons to do his number?"

Hesitantly, young Berlin said, "I've been standing here mentally working on a new song. If you don't mind listening, Mr. Block, I'd like your opinion of it."

Block scratched out a room with a piano and listened. "Just sit there—don't go away," Block yelled, "I'll be right back." Moments later he was back with George M. "Listen to this kid, Georgie! You're looking for a closing number to the minstrel first part? This kid has just played a song whose lyrics and rhythm are all minstrel! I've never heard anything like it in my life. Go ahead Irving! Play that song again!"

Berlin did a reprise. The words and music filled the room and brought about the greatest tribute of all—one master spontaneously shouting his acclaim for another master's work. ,

"That's it," cried Cohan. "It sounds like it was written by the man who invented minstrels himself." Thus, a great song received its baptismal. Soon its modest creator was leading the Frolics through "Alexander's Ragtime Band!"

Friar Al Jolson had a favorite song that started, "I don't care who writes the laws of the nation—as long as I can sing its popular songs." Well, a passel of songwriting Friars supplied him for years:

> Lou Silvers with "April Showers"
> Sam M. Lewis with "Sittin' on Top of the World"
> Harry Woods with "Red, Red Robin"
> Bud De Sylva with "Look for the Silver Lining"

So many top songs were the gifts of gifted Friar members:

> Harry von Tilzer: "I Want a Girl (Just like the Girl That
> Married Dear Old Dad)"
> Gene Buck: "Hello Frisco"
> Harry Carroll: "Chasing Rainbows"
> Jimmy Monaco: "You Made Me Love You"
> Nat Ayer: "Oh, You Beautiful Doll"
> Ray Henderson: "The Best Things in Life Are Free"
> Victor Herbert: "Kiss Me Again" and, of course,
> "The Friars Song"

One of the celebrated nights in Friars history is the ASCAP house party put on by Stanley Adams, president of the American Society of Composers and Publishers, and Lou Alter, one of their brightest lights. Stanley did the overture:

"Ladies and Gentlemen: Tonight you will hear some of ASCAP's outstanding writers playing and singing one or two of their great songs.

"I am sure you are fully acquainted with the attendant difficulties in writing a Broadway musical comedy. And yet, by using just some of the titles of the songs written by these composers, we can ad-lib a pretty workable libretto. For example:

"It seems that Benny Davis's 'Margie,' while under the influence of Lou Alter's 'Manhattan Serenade,' met Abe Olman's 'Johnny,' while strolling along on Jimmy McHugh's 'Sunny Side of the Street.'

"According to Johnny Burke, 'Johnny' looked at 'Margie' and said 'Suddenly It's Spring' and I want to be with you 'Sunday, Monday and Always.' She said, as related by Wolfie Gilbert and Abel Baer, 'Don't Wake Me Up, Let Me Dream.'

"On the day of the wedding there was such a tremendous crowd that Eli Basse tells me 'The Groom Couldn't Get In' but he finally did and after the ceremony, we are told by Harry Woods, Irving Caesar, and Mitchell Parish, they went to a little spot where 'The Moon Comes Over the Mountain,' enjoyed 'Tea for Two,' listened to a 'Red, Red Robin,' and for a long time had 'Stardust' in their hearts.

"But one day 'Johnny' was introduced to Lou Alter's 'Dolores' and Richard Rodgers remarked that 'Johnny's Heart Stood Still.'

"When 'Margie' heard about this turn of events, Arthur Schwartz heard her say 'I Guess I'll Have to Change My Plans' but I don't feel too bad or sad by it because 'I'm Just Wild About Harry.'"

I just want to add "What a Difference a Day Makes" was written by Stanley Adams when he was "Waiting for the Robert E. Lee" written by veteran Friar Wolfie Gilbert on his way to "Swanee" by Irving Caesar who said "Happy Days Are Here Again" by Milton Ager and Jack Yellen if you "Take Me in Your Arms" by Mitchell Parish and "I Think I'm Going Out of My Mind," which may or may not be the title of a song but I think it's happening to me.

16

Thanks for the Memories

Unless you had heartburn, you don't remember every course at every dinner whether at your mother-in-law's or if you're putting up 100 bucks a shot at a Friars roast. But there are some things over the years that do stick to the ribs:

Like the time the Friars skewered Sophie Tucker. The "Last of the Red Hot Mammas" was the first lady ever to get the golden shaft at the proverbial stag roast.

The Friars broke with tradition and honored Sophie on the celebration of her Golden Jubilee in show business, fifty years of great entertainment from a great lady. The year 1953 was a good year. On the dais surrounding the First Lady of the Friars were Milton Berle, Georgie Jessel, Frank Sinatra, Smith and Dale, Jack E. Leonard, Dean Harry Delf, Jesse Block, Myron Cohen, Abel Green, and Earl Wilson, besides Benny Fields, Jack Carter, Red Buttons, Meyer Davis, Henny Youngman, and scores of other show-biz notables in the audience.

Sophie said, "This is the first time I've been in a room alone with enough men. The hell of it is, it comes so late."

It was Frank Sinatra who said it all in a parody to Sophie, written by Milton Berle, to the tune of "Mother" ("Put them all together, they spell mother"):

> S is for the sweetness that's within her.
> O is for the oldies that she sings.
> P is for the people that adore her.
> H is for the happiness she brings.
> I is for the ideals that she lives by.
> E is for her endless curtain calls.

Put them all together they spell Sophie
The only Friar without balls
And We're not certain
The only Friar without balls.

The biggest laugh humorist Irvin S. Cobb ever got, in his own opinion, was at the expense of his bosom friend, Will Rogers, during a Friars Club dinner.

The newspaperman, short-story writer, radio personality, after-dinner speaker, and movie actor is proudest of this one great ad-lib. Will Hays, the movie czar, had just told how Will Rogers, an unknown Oklahoma boy, had come to New York, adding: "It didn't take this town long to find out there was something under his old black slouch hat besides hair." Whereupon Cobb jumped up from his chair and interjected, "I'm awfully glad Will Hays said what he just did because it's high time somebody in this country spoke a kind word for dandruff."

One of the great Friars affairs was the night the needler got needled. A couple of thousand showed at the Americana Hotel on April 20, 1975, to see Don "The Killer" Rickles get the hot seat.

Johnny Carson, in his capacity (which is about half a gallon) as toastmaster, started it all by saying: "Don is such a family man he gave his mother a Florida swimming pool with a shark in it." Dr. Joyce Brothers said, "He is the kind to help old ladies halfway across the street." George Kirby said, "The only thing that Rickles knows about brotherhood is that his brother is a hood." Pat Henry said, "Rickles was born an only twin—the other one lived."

Morey Amsterdam embraced him: "Folks, you know Don Rickles —the original Rat Patrol." Jan Murray noted: "Rickles, our guest of honor—what little he has left—is the man about whom Hitler said, 'From him I could learn.'" Jack Carter: "It was Don who taught the Arabs how to fight dirty." Red Buttons: "Don married a good girl—a sentimental girl. She saw a sign 'Help the Handicapped'—so she married him."

The topper that will live with Don for a long time was Milton Berle's adoring line: "What can you say about Rickles that hasn't been said about hemorrhoids?"

The Joe E. Lewis X-rated luncheon at the Copa on October 24, 1958, will be remembered by everyone present that day, long after they forget about sex.

Super-stud Errol Flynn, who in those days was reputed to use his tools more often than the Roto-Rooter man, was the target of the afternoon. Every comic in town hung his jokes on his procreative organ. Toastmaster Jack E. Leonard started it: "Even as an infant he grabbed for the nurse instead of the bottle." Joe E. remarked, "He's real broad-minded. In fact, he thinks of nothing else." Red Buttons mentioned, "He can read girls like a book, and he likes to read in bed." Flynn had a fixed grin all through the roast.

When Errol was asked to speak he said simply: "I admit sex is the most fun you can have without laughing. When I was seven years old I *bleeped* a duck.

"Sex is so popular because it's centrally located. Now I suppose you're wondering why I was smiling all through this luncheon. Let me assure you that it wasn't the gags I heard today. While all you guys were making jokes, there was a redhead under the table that was *bleeping* my *bleep*."

Walter Goldstein will always remember the 1960 dinner for Dinah Shore because of his "friend" Liberace. Executive Directors Carl Timin and Walter Goldstein were the team putting on the show, which is never easy—getting the guest of honor, inviting the stars, setting up the dinner, arranging the seating, publicity, setting up the charities, and a hundred other acid-producing experiences.

Walter was assigned the task of taking care of Liberace. He's still trying to figure out what he did in his past life to deserve this honor. First of all, Liberace insisted on a special piano that he always uses for his appearances, for pay or for benefits.

Who knows why this was the only piano in the whole world that would satisfy Liberace. Maybe the keys came from the tusks of pure virgin elephants. Maybe the wood was polished, buffed, and licked by blind Belgian nuns. We only know that this was the only piano in the whole world on which Liberace would sit down and dreidel.

I guess it wasn't too much to ask since Liberace was doing it for free—except that the dinner was Sunday night and Walter found out about the problem Sunday morning. It took a lot of connections and a couple of hundred phone calls to get the Steinway people to open the store—and a couple of hundred extra bucks and a few ulcers to get the truckers to schlep the piano to the Waldorf—at time and a half, double on Sunday. Naturally, they left the Steinway on the floor under the stage. But Lee wanted it *on*stage—facing east toward Mecca or Coney Island—on a 45-degree angle, with a special bench and a red sequined seat.

Now it was Walter's job to get the union guys to lift it onstage—

at triple-and-a-half Sunday scale—plus hernia insurance. All of it was accomplished by curtain time—just before Liberace made his entrance.

Walter was tired but happy as Lee was introduced and walked to center stage where "the" piano stood at the right angle with the candelabra in its special place. Liberace passed the piano, nodded to the orchestra, and went into his soft-shoe dance, never touching the piano, never even looking at it, and walked offstage.

Let's put it this way—Goldstein didn't write Liberace no fan letters.

The 1956 roast of Ed Sullivan at the Waldorf was too well done, but the Port Chester, New York, kid was made of special stuff. He was born stamped U.S. Prime. He could take it. Ed was the first nonpro to get the Friar treatment—unless you called his MC'ing professional. Actually, he was a columnist and the editor of his television show. As Fred Allen said: "He isn't exactly a master of ceremonies—he's a pointer"—but the nicest, kindest, and most charitable man on Broadway.

In an era when columnists like Walter Winchell, Dorothy Kilgallen, Westbrook Pegler, Louella Parsons, and others were poison pen pals, Ed was sugar and spice and everything nice.

A couple of thousand pounds of comedians showed up to unleash some of the material they couldn't use on the Ed Sullivan Show, which was strictly family entertainment. The only reason Smiley graciously submitted to this vivisection was to raise $100,000 or more for his favorite charities.

Joe E. Lewis, who took the job as toastmaster because he thought all a toastmaster has to do is drink toasts all night, was really ready by his third bottle of toasts. He introduced Ed: "He can light up a whole room—just by leaving it. He started as a greeter at Forest Lawn Cemetery."

Oscar Hammerstein, Sol Hurok, Joan Crawford, Governor Ribicoff, Robert Mitchum, Edward R. Murrow, John Daly, Risë Stevens, James Petrillo were some of the faces who were there to honor Ed. After they took their bows we went to work. Jack E. Leonard said: 'They kid you too much, Ed. They kid you about your looks. They kid you about your personality. But I don't—I don't think you have any."

Jan Murray noted: "Ed knows what the public likes and some day he may give it to them." Jack Carter said: "Sullivan looks great. He should be president. He belongs up there on Mount Rushmore next to Jefferson, Washington, and Lincoln. They don't even have to chisel him out of stone—he's ready right now."

Red Buttons explained: "I wouldn't say Ed has no personality, but his TV show is in color and he comes out in black and white." Steve Allen showed his love: "Ed is a great showman. After all, he's been on TV for years—and I finally figured out the reason for his success—he's never improved."

Phil Silvers was warm: "Ed Sullivan has taken some of the biggest stars and made unknowns of them." And my favorite comedian, Joey Adams, finished it all up: "You can sum up Ed Sullivan's career in one word—'lucky.'"

The year was 1955 and it was the fiftieth anniversary of the Friars. The guests of honor were the hottest act in show business, Martin and Lewis. As Jan Murray said: "Isn't it wonderful that a Jewish boy and a Gentile boy should be such successful partners, and what is more amazing the Gentile boy has the nose job."

Ringmaster Milton Berle introduced every star in town who came to honor Dean and Jerry, from Sam Levinson, Robert Q. Lewis, Bobby Clark, Buddy Hackett, Steve Allen, and Robert Merrill to Joe DiMaggio, Sammy Davis, Jr., and Joey Adams and Al Kelly. Milton cracked: "If a bomb hit the Waldorf tonight, Pinky Lee would become the biggest star in town."

The drama backstage, however, was greater than all the hysteria in the ballroom. The big stars of the evening—Martin and Lewis— were breaking up. They were never funnier when they finally got to the microphone and started to throw lines at each other—but offstage they weren't talking at all. Only they knew that this was a farewell party to each other.

Everything was going great. Robert Merrill remembered the words to "The Star Spangled Banner," Eddie Fisher hit high notes he hadn't reached since he was a production singer at the Copa, Benny Fields and Blossom Seeley were appropriately nostalgic, and even Mayor Robert F. Wagner got his share of laughs. But the spotlight was on a fluorescent creature sitting next to me on the dais, Marilyn Monroe.

No matter what was going on at the microphone, all eyes were focused on the undulating, pulsating, throbbing Marilyn. Henny Youngman got an ovation just because Marilyn Monroe hoisted herself to adjust her gown. Buddy Hackett stopped the show when Miss Monroe bent over to fix whatever it was she fixed. Bobby Clark got cheers when Marilyn just pulled up the spaghetti straps on her gown.

The big thrill of the evening came when Sammy Davis, Jr., got to the microphone. Even before he started to sing, Marilyn got up again and started to wriggle past him and with all her movable parts moving in opposite directions made for the exit. "Excuse me," she whispered in that voice that only dogs could hear, "I'm going to the little girl's room," and out she slunk.

Naturally, every eye, ear, nose, and throat was pointed in her direction. Half the females in the audience, including a few queens I know, suddenly felt the urge to go at the same moment. All I can tell you is the Hebrews in the Bible placed second to this mass exodus.

I didn't mind following Sammy Davis on the bill. What did bother me was that Marilyn Monroe had a bigger audience in the ladies' room than I had in the ballroom.

George Jessel has some great memories of the club he loves best:

In the year 1919, I had an ambition realized when Louis Silvers, the composer and musical director (who had taught me to play six chords on the piano when I was ten), phoned me backstage at B. F. Keith's Alhambra to tell me that I had become a member of the Friars, he having sponsored me.

I remember that I cut my act by at least four minutes, ran to the 125th Street subway station in New York to get down to the club, the great Friars Monastery on 48th Street. For there I would see the theatrical idols I worshiped, George M. Cohan, William Collier, Sam Bernard, Irving Berlin, Harry Fox, Frank Tinney, Louis Mann, Walter C. Kelly, "Gentleman Jim" Corbett, Will Rogers, Enrico Caruso, Jimmy Walker, Harry Cooper, William Morris, and maybe even President Woodrow Wilson.

I walked in with the awe of an "untouchable" entering the Taj Mahal. I stood at the doorway, near the bar in the Grill Room, and the first words I heard were: "Caruso, you are a schmuck!" The reason for this remark I found out later, was that the great tenor had made a faux pas in pinching a fat lady's bottom in the Bronx Zoo and it was all over the newspapers. The great comedian Sam Bernard, while everybody was kidding the great tenor, raised his glass and bellowed: "Caruso, you are a schmuck!"

The years have been on, so many, since then! Many glasses have been lifted, and many men have been called "schmucks!" In the years that followed I became the dean, and then the abbot of the New York Friars, and remained so until I came to live in California.

In 1946, I founded the Friars of California. Since then, the club has flourished, and has proved to be the most generous group of men of any social club of its time. And like the Friars of old, we have no inhibitions about what we say or what we think in the confines of the Monastery. And history repeats itself! Only a short time ago, I too was in the papers about pinching or—something!—a girl! And as I walked into the club one night, Frank Sinatra said: "Jessel, you're a schmuck!" Yes, history does repeat itself!

There will always be men who, because of girls, will get their names in the newspapers, and so there'll always be "schmucks!" And may the Lord see to it that there'll always be Friars!

It was at a Friars roastimonial to the undefeated world's heavyweight champ Rocky Marciano that I met the most unforgettable character in the history of the club, Solly Violinsky, violinist, pianist, songwriter, and wit—and out of work in all of them.

"I'm a champ, too," he said to Rocky. " "Oh, are you?" Marciano asked. He didn't seem too frightened facing the innocent-looking, bespectacled, quiet-appearing man. "Yeah, I'm the champ at laying off. I've laid off under four presidents—in all forms of show business except Cinerama—and give me time, I'll add that." Violinsky admitted, "I have had my violin in hock so long—my pawnbroker plays it better than I do."

Rocky tried to be interested. "Back in the old days," Solly continued, "I made big money—the bills were twice as large in those days."

There was the occasion when ASCAP, the American Society of Composers and Publishers, determined that the affluence of the huge organization be expressed in a gold pin to be worn in the buttonholes of the coats of the membership. ASCAP prexy Stanley Adams had the pins mailed to all the songwriters from Irving Berlin to Irving Caesar, Mitchell Parrish, George Gershwin, and Solly Violinsky. "Very enthused over pin," wired Violinsky, "but at present have no coat—please advise."

Solly liked to recall his terrific triumph in England in 1910. During the coronation of King George V he had an apartment overlooking the procession. As the royal carriage passed, he threw open the window and played his violin. Next day he ran advertisements about the great Solly Violinsky "who played before the king and queen."

Violinsky fell and broke his leg some time back. "Luckily I have insurance," he said between sobs. "Wonderful, what kind?" Earl Wilson asked. "Fire and theft," said Solly.

Once Violinsky was asked if he was going to fly to Binghamton, his hometown. "Fly to Binghamton?" he hollered, "who the hell is in a hurry to get to Binghamton?"

I remember the time Violinsky was standing in front of the club depressed after a bad day at the track. Jay C. Flippen rushed out with, "I gotta run—this is my bridge night." Solly moaned, "Mine too, let's jump together."

Jesse Block introduced him to John A. Coleman who was just elected to the board of directors of the New York Telephone Company. Violinsky eyed Coleman with interest: "That job of yours is twice as good now that phone calls are a dime."

Coleman laughed: "I see that you follow the telephone company operations very closely, Mr. Violinsky."

Solly nodded: "In self-defense. For years when phone calls were a nickel, my agent called me once a week. Now that the rates have been raised to a dime, he doesn't call me at all. This is a great improvement—I now lay off direct."

"Is it profitable being a wit?" I once asked the great Violinsky. "Twice as profitable as being a half-wit," Solly said.

The Bob Hope dinner brought out 1,500 people at a cost of fifty bucks a head prompting the former Leslie Townes Hope of England to crack, "No man can be this great, but you've finally convinced me. I never felt so humble nor so deductible." Thirty of his favored charities fought to participate and to say a word from the dais but Hope himself said, "You can't entertain people with plaques" so the proceeds were divided among four: United Cerebral Palsy, the Boy Scouts of America, U.S.O., and the Friars Club Relief Fund.

The onetime legit actor in such antique B.C. (Before Crosby) Broadway musicals as *Roberta* and *Red, Hot and Blue* brought out the biggest. Hope drew Missouri Senator Stuart Symington, Major General Emmett "Rosie" O'Donnell, Danny Kaye who somebody gift-wrapped as Hans Jewish Andersen, Thomas Burke, the mayor of his hometown, Cleveland, and such elder statesmen as octogenarian Bernard Baruch who arrived late and departed early, the then eighty-year-old Adolph Zukor who began the motion-picture industry with Sarah Bernhardt and ended it up in Paramount with Betty Hutton and "the man who reflects Southern Comfort—the Kentuckian who wasn't born but was bonded in bourbon, the

Thanks for the memories.

former Vice-President of the United States of America Alben Barkley." Those names may live forever but about those tuxedos! Some reviewer wrote later: "A few of the dinner jackets looked like they were cut by McKinley's tailor!"

Even Hope who referred to himself as "former dean, proctor, herald, doorman, and schnook of the West Coast branch of the Friars" made mention of the seniority of the dais: "It's wonderful to see so many of my old friends . . . I never knew I had so many friends that old."

Since Hope was just an average American who earned about $3 million a year and was an NBC star it was only fitting that the NBC biggies should show. They may have been a little lighter in years than his other pals but heavyweights they were for sure. RCA President Frank Folsom took this Jesselism: "It is told that one of his employees said, 'Sir, I would like tomorrow off. It is my twenty-fifth wedding anniversary,' and Folsom said to the fellow, 'Okay, but must I have this trouble with you every twenty-five years?'"

Frank White managed his bow after "and now the president of NBC—as of Friday, 9:51 P.M. EST."

What with the guest of honor being a sacred cow in show business the weightier names almost outnumbered the wittier ones. The mayor of the City of New York, the Honorable Vincent Impellitteri, smiled through, "I hope you stay in office, Mr. Mayor. But, of course, I come from Los Angeles." Motion-picture czar Eric Johnston was lauded as the brilliant man "who just learned the secret of how the Italians got that realistic look in their films—they use a dirty lens."

Paul Ash conducted the music, Benny Davis composed special lyrics, the Met's Robert Merrill sang as did PFC Eddie Fisher whose accompanist was Hugo Winterhalter no less, Tony and Sally De-Marco, the dancing greats danced great, and Betty and Jane Kean brought their act over from the Copa. The hit of the evening was Fred Allen:

> Most big dinners start with the selection of a guest of honor. The Friars work differently. They are afraid to plan a dinner until they know that Jessel is available. If Georgie can make it, then they send out to Hollywood for a guest because most of the New York Friars are out of work. And how would it look to give a big dinner for an unemployed guest of honor. Mr. Jessel, of course, is banquet insurance. Lindy's is sending out a four-dollar dinner and as it's delivered Jessel says a few words in the hall at the open door. In fact, he's so eager to speak that afterwards you never know whether the sounds you hear are some abdominal disturbance or more of Mr. Jessel.
>
> About the guest of honor. I feel there is nothing any of us can say about Mr. Hope that he has not already said about himself. He was born in London into a family of seven boys. Rather a large family by British standards. The British are so reserved, you know. They seldom get close enough together to breathe and the race is perpetuated by foreigners and through correspondence mainly with the Colonies. Little Leslie was so poor that he used a bicycle pump to blow his kipper up into a bloater.
>
> The family came to America to raise their Hopes and I met Leslie in New York in a boardinghouse where room and board was a dollar a day. The room was a crypt with a transom on it and as for the board there was a plaque in the dining room where Duncan Hines had fallen. The hotel was so cold that the actors were able to keep warm only from the heartburn they got from eating the food. The whole place was filthy. The only thing you could see

through the windows was an eclipse. Even the mice had athlete's foot.

Mr. Hope began in vaudeville with a double act but he told his jokes so fast his partner couldn't get her lines in. He immediately became a monologist. He went into musical comedy but he couldn't tolerate the intermissions. They forced him to get off the stage between acts. Movies had no intermissions so he could be on all the time so he immediately made for Hollywood. Hollywood was started many years ago by a writer who went West with a cliché. Hollywood is a place where a person works all his life to become recognized, then wears dark glasses so nobody will know who he is. Hollywood is where the Bank of America has its president who sits in an office with nothing but a giant cuspidor. If you are an independent producer and you are going to make a picture with spit, you have to see him.

With the many complimentary things that have been said about our guest of honor tonight I am sure that this season the grass will grow green from the Waldorf to New Rochelle. Money has never gone to Mr. Hope's head. Most of it has gone to the government. Mr. Hope's fame is assured, Westbrook Pegler spoke well of him. Mr. Hope has written two books which proves that his flair for the trite has been manifested on more than one occasion. . . ."

Fred Allen stopped the banquet cold. The guests were revived only with Milton Berle who called Hope "America's second greatest comedian" and called Jessel "such a skillful toastmaster that he invites girls up to his apartment just to see his menus" and spoke of Fred Allen as "a wonderful goy."

When Hope rose to thank everybody he said, "I don't know what to say. Everything's already been said. Will somebody please run down to Ruby Foo's and get me a fortune cookie to read. I loved what Fred Allen had to say. I now feel I was run over by Sophie Tucker. I was cut up more than RKO. And, of course, I love Milton. I love to sit home and watch him on TV and see how my jokes are doing."

Then he introduced his wife, his writers, his press agent, told his brothers Fred, George, and Iver to stand up and take a bow with, "But don't stay up very long. Remember you're on the lam" and segued into the humble bit. He thanked everybody but the pro in the men's room. I tell you the truth the Bob Hope dinner was such a great evening it couldn't have been better unless it was in honor of me!

I'll remember the Humphrey Bogart X-rated luncheon for two

things—Lauren Bacall and Charles Coburn. Historian Ed Weiner started by reading a telegram to Bogart from Clark Gable: "Congratulations on your comeback—thought you were too old to come again."

There were no women allowed, so Red Buttons, the toastmaster, introduced a taped message from Humphrey Bogart's wife Lauren Bacall: "You rat bastard—I know I'm not allowed to attend a stag—but what the hell can the Friars call me that you haven't called me?

"I remember your former girl friend leaning out the window yelling, 'Hump-free Hump-free' and twenty guys ran up to see her.

"I just want the guys at the lunch to know the truth. Bogey thinks he's such a tough guy that he wakes me up three or four times a night and asks me to hold his gun."

Red Buttons, in introducing the distinguished actor Charles Coburn, said: "He's such a gentleman—he always removes his monocle when he goes to the bathroom to take a *bleep*." Coburn answered: "That's not the reason I remove my monocle—it's just that I'm ashamed to look down."

Another great memory of the Friars is the lunch in honor of Jack E. Leonard that was MC'd by Jack E. himself. I still don't know how the guys got their lines in, but they did:

George Kirby praised Jack for his integration activities: "In Chicago in his younger days, Leonard was the first white man to go into a black ghetto—and he mugged two black men."

David Frost said: "Jack E. has the sardonic wit of Kate Smith, the personality of Arthur Godfrey, the great taste of Linda Lovelace, and the sex appeal of Tiny Tim."

Alan King disclosed that as a kid he had two idols: Abe Reles of Murder Incorporated and Jack E. Leonard. "Why the hell they threw Reles out the window and not Jack E.—I'll never know."

Harry Hershfield said: "I don't like to tangle with Leonard because no matter where you hit him he claims foul—because he's all *bleep*."

Joe E. Lewis: "That Jack E. sure has a sharp tongue—that's what that girl in Philly told me."

Robert Merrill read a telegram from Rudolf Bing of the Met: "Since the loss a few years ago of two of my great thin singers, Lauritz Melchior and Helen Traubel, and also after hearing a recording of yours recently—we have decided, if you could *bleep* Maria Callas in a rowboat—you got the job."

Joey Bishop said: "Put your teeth in backwards, and bite yourself in the throat."

Jack E. was so overtaken with all this loving sentiment he said: "This is a great club and a great bunch of guys. We ought to have a membership drive—to drive out some of the membership."

George Raft was honored by the Friars at luncheons in New York and California. It proved that even at seventy-nine he's still a draw. Although he would be the first to tell you, he can't draw as fast as he used to.

I introduced Don Rickles as "the greatest wit since Arthur Murray." Don was sweet about Raft: "George is a New York boy that made good. Fifty years ago he came to California for arthritis—he finally got it."

Frank Sinatra and his pal Pat Henry showed to pay their disrespect for Raft. Pat cracked: "Sinatra always gives me fifteen minutes to warm up an audience. You can't warm up a lasagna in fifteen minutes.

"But it's a pleasure being here for George. Just like Sinatra, wherever he appears he draws the cream of society—only the best people. Take that table over there. That crowd represents a total of 324 years off for good behavior."

Or the Perry Como dinner in 1957. MC Phil Silvers said: "Perry accepted this honor because he thought the Friars was a branch of the Church."

Phil noted that the Emmy Awards voted Perry the most outstanding personality over some pretty tough competition. Like Bishop Sheen, for example. "The Bishop was expected here tonight but he is over at St. Patrick's asking 'Why?'"

Phil said, "We had expected Bishop Sheen tonight, but instead we have another Bishop, Joey. Perry wanted him here because he thought he was a real bishop. He should know that Joey wanted to be a rabbi—but how would it sound 'Rabbi Bishop?'"

Bishop said simply: "I don't like you, Como. You and your nice, quiet, religious, simple, sweet manner. How would you like a rap in the mouth?"

The Alan King dinner at the Waldorf-Astoria benefited the Martin Luther King, Jr., Foundation and the Robert F. Kennedy Foundation. Naturally, Coretta King and all the Kennedys got into the act. The dais had Ethel, Pat Lawford, Jean and Stephen Smith, and Joan and Teddy cheering and roasting Alan.

All the liberal senators showed to embrace the liberal comic, from Teddy Kennedy to Thomas Eagleton, Philip A. Hart, Frank Moss, and almost Senator Astronaut Colonel John Glenn to Senators George McGovern, John Tunney, and Mayor John Lindsay.

Of course, the liberal jokes all came out. Godfrey Cambridge told of the California earthquake: "My house slid into a restricted area."

Toastmaster David Frost introduced George Jessel: "He gets up every morning and looks in the *Times*. If his name is not in the obituary column—he calls up a dame."

Jessel said: "You know what a conservative is? That's a liberal who's been mugged."

Pat Henry best remembered Alan's liberal views and his work for liberal causes: "As an example of King's social directions, Alan always changes places with his chauffeur while riding through Harlem in his Rolls-Royce."

17

The Sunshine Boys George Burns and Walter Matthau

The Sunshine Boys spread it around pretty good. The roast in their honor at the Americana Hotel on the night of April 10, 1975, made the Friars charity fund richer by some $100,000, which was distributed to dozens of needy organizations such as the Actors' Fund, Catholic Actors' Guild, Actors' Temple, Fight for Sight, City of Hope, Will Rogers Memorial, U.S.O. camp shows, organizations, and people as long and far as the sunshine lasted.

This was the first time Burns and Matthau worked as a team. George had started at the age of seven singing on ferryboats. "Sometimes people put pennies in my hat," George remembers. "Sometimes they threw me overboard. I got so I could sing better with water in my mouth. Actually, even if they threw me overboard I couldn't drown—there was too much garbage."

He met Gracie Allen in 1923 and became the top half of Burns and Allen. "I got top billing," he says, "because I didn't want anyone to know I didn't do anything. Gracie carried me along."

Walter Matthau wore a cap all through this black-tie dinner in their honor. "They shaved my head for the *Sunshine Boys* picture and since I'm very vain I won't be seen bald. My mother told me, 'Walter, don't go out without something covering your head.'" So he sat there all night like a Yeshiva boy or a Talmudic student waiting to make his Bar Mitzvah speech.

Mayor Abraham Beame started the roast: "I'm really sorry that my schedule won't permit me to stay through the evening but I'm sure Uncle Miltie will understand. It will be hard to forego hearing Milton Berle tell me that I'm looking great—I took off a little height—but it won't be the first time part of his audience walked out.

"I see a lot of familiar faces here. And when I think of the city's money problems, I want to say to Henny Youngman, take New York—*please!* I want you to know, Henny, that I bought that line at a discount from another show-biz guy, John Lindsay.

"Well, here we are to honor the Sunshine Boys, or is it 'The Odd Couple?' George Burns and Gracie Matthau. They've brought laughter and tears to generations of audiences. Matthau's dramatic performance and George's jokes have brought laughter and tears —in that order.

"George Burns got an early start in show business. When Moses spoke, George used to hold the cue stones.

"I understand Walter got a terrific deal for his movie *The Taking of Pelham One, Two, Three.* He got paid in tokens."

Mayor Beame presented Burns and Matthau with the keys to the city and left—probably to change the locks.

Dean Buddy Howe then welcomed the Friars, the members of the dais, David Tebet, the NBC VP who was executive chairman of the dinner, William B. Williams, chairman, Walter Goldstein, executive director, and Sherry Wolf for creating *The Sunshine Boys* journal cover painting that brought about $30,000 more to the Friars charity fund, then the Friars song with special lyrics by Sammy Cahn: "Sell your rockers, welcome these altercockers." Toastmaster Alan King took it from there: "Thanks to Dean Buddy Howe for his great work for the Friars. Buddy, as you know, is the VP at G.A.C., which merged with C.M.A., and C.M.A. bought out I.F.A., and then G.A.C. and C.M.A. and I.F.A. combined into a conglomerate affectionately known in the trade as S-H-I-T.

"This party is in honor of two men who have brought sunshine into our lives. Walter may not be aware that Burns is so charitable and generous. All you got to do is approach him with a sad story. Any broken-down, busted-out actor can walk up to George Burns and ask for anything and George will take out his wallet and show him a picture of his sister Goldie.

"I want Walter to know that our Abbot Frank Sinatra wanted to be here for him. He couldn't make it tonight because he made it twice this afternoon and was awfully tired."

Alan King next introduced Norm Crosby as "the great American historic who has overcome many physical handicaps. Number one he talks funny. But he overcame that by being deaf. A man who didn't have his first sexual experience until he was forty-two years old. It took his wife that long to figure out what the hell he was asking for. I give you a man with great stigma and flux, a lovely man, Mr. Norm Crosby."

"Thank you very much, Alan. Thank you, ladies and gentlemen. Those of you who perhaps are not familiar with the idiot secrecies of our business may not realize that it is a very proud honor to be selected as the first speaker at a testicle such as this," burbled Norm.

"This is a great evening. Look around you. Take a look, bi-sexually, around the room, and feel the stigma that is present in this building. I have been to many Friar dinners but I say this honestly, and without fear of contraception—this is by far the most migraine perfunctory group that I ever sat with. I really mean that. I don't know if you noticed it—but when you came in this room, there is an aura of reek in this building that comes from these two men.

"You come to pay tribute, my friends, to two gentlemen. Men of depth and perversion who sit here. Men whose fame extends from the most ethereal to the most venereal concept of the world of drama. I really mean that and yet I say this with all due respect and to my fellow Friars and to the procurers who have arranged this evening.

"To George Burns—it's amazing that a man of his unlimited age can have the sex life that he has. I mean that. He does everything twice. He makes love twice. He's always cool during the first session —but the second time makes him perspire a little bit—that's because the first one is in January and the second one in August.

"To Walter Matthau who's sitting there drinking his Geritol on the Rocks—I quote the Old Testament—or Methuselah who had the oldest testaments of them all—age gives you wisdom—it gives you responsibility, and it gives you irregularity. That's why I would really like to say honestly that I have such profound respect and affection for both these gentlemen. I am very proud to be just a small part of this delightful evening. Thank you very much."

Jesse Block of the legendary team of Block and Sully was next with his nostalgia and reminiscences. As Jesse admitted: "My wife says the only thing I can do today is reminisce."

Alan took over again: "I should like to introduce Johnny Carson —but I am forced to introduce Henny Youngman. The Friars are grateful to Henny because he has never turned down an invitation

—even when he didn't receive one. A man who started out as a small-time nightclub comedian, and never lived up to his promise —take Henny Youngman—*please*."

"One thing about you, Alan," Henny opened, "you have no ulcer, but you're a carrier. Now there's Milton Berle. One thing about Milton, he's never lost an enemy. A few words about Walter Matthau. This man has had very little education. When he was twelve, the extent of his education, he was hit by a school bus. He has screwed up more pictures than Jack Lemmon who is here tonight. Jack was supposed to play the part of a terrorist. They sent him to blow up a car, he burned his lips on the exhaust pipe.

"This is George Burns's first picture in thirty-six years. He screwed up the first one. He was supposed to play the part of a rapist. They put him in a police lineup and when the girls walked in he said, 'That's her.' Good luck, Walter and George."

Milton Berle was introduced next as "Mr. Television—or Mr. Tuesday Night—which is what his wife Ruth still calls him—the two funniest words in the business—Milton Berle."

Berle started on Henny: "Following Youngman is like asking Linda Lovelace to sing 'Whistle While You Work.' Henny, you are to comedy what Ernest Borgnine is to tap dancing. And I'm glad Alan King did his usual job tonight—unfortunately.

"But I'm very, very glad to be here tonight to honor my closest friends, Walter Mathews and the late George Appleby. I'd like to tell you how I happened to be here. Walter Goldstein called me on the phone in California and said, 'Milton, Matthau and Burns are having an affair at the Americana.' I said, 'I know they're queer, but in front of everybody? It's ridiculous.'

"It isn't easy being selected as the guest of honor for a Friars dinner—first you have to be listed in the phone book. Remember, I'm the abbot emeritus, which is about as important as being the comedy consultant on the 'Joe Franklin Show.'

"It's exciting being back in New York. Our idea of a thrilling evening in Beverly Hills is to go over to Burns's house and watch him wake up his leg—or listen to Gabby Hayes make obscene phone calls to Jane Withers. One night we had a lot of fun at Kirk Douglas's house. We threw a white sheet over Totie Fields. We showed motion pictures on her behind.

"As abbot emeritus I want to say something. Some biggies couldn't be here but they send their best to our guests of honor. Burt Reynolds, he would have been here but he had an accident.

He crossed his legs very quickly—he's in critical condition. Danny Thomas couldn't be here—he's at Brentano's autographing Bibles. Sinatra did promise to bring his whole family here for our next dinner. And that way we'll get to meet the son, the daughter, and the Holy Ghost.

"Now for the guest of honor. First I speak about my very dear friend Nat Birnbaum—George Burns. I love this man. I must say, George, Mother Nature has been very good to you—but, unfortunately, Father Time sure kicked the *hell* out of you.

"George's biggest sex thrill now is when he's being frisked at airports. I don't know if he's eighty. I really can't tell how old George is—but when he was circumcised they used a stone knife.

"Now we come to the Academy Award winner Walter Matthau. May I say, Walter, I've never liked you. But you are a fantastic actor. You've told me that many times. You've got it up here. I've seen him in the steam room and he certainly hasn't got it down there.

"It's been a great thrill to honor Walter and George—they are really the 'Sunshine Boys'—and may you live to be as old as my act . . ."

Jessel, who started the Friars roasts many years ago, was particularly sentimental and dedicated the evening to Smith and Dale and Burns and Matthau and the Friars of New York: "Make new friends, but keep the old. Those are silver, these are gold. And new-made friendships like new wine, age must mellow and refine. But friendships that have stood the test of time and change are surely best. Brows may wrinkle, hair grow gray. Old friendships never know decay. So cherish friendship when you're best. New is good. But old is best. Make new friends, but keep the old. Those are silver, these are gold.

"God bless the memory of Smith and Dale. God bless the genius of Neil Simon who has written this play about them, *The Sunshine Boys*. And these fine artists Matthau and Burns. God bless the Friars. God bless America."

Maureen Stapleton said: "With all his diseases, that Walter Matthau will live forever—the prayers of his bookmakers will keep him alive."

Jimmy Joyce told about his old Irish aunt in Boston who used to take him to see George Burns at the old Keith Boston Theatre. One day she went to confession and said to the priest, "I got thirteen kids, don't you think it's about time I took the pill?" He said, "You

can't do that, that's against our religion. Have you tried the rhythm system?" She said, "Where the hell am I going to get an orchestra at two o'clock in the morning?"

George Kirby said: "I tried to figure what there is about George Burns. What makes him different? Well, let's see. He's an old vaude-villian, a singer, he's short, Jewish, but then so is Sammy Davis. But let me say something about the other guy. That Walter Matthau has a gift for comedy—he should have exchanged it for a pair of paja-mas."

Jack Lemmon said: "I'm not going to try to be funny—why spoil the format of this evening?"

In the old days of vaudeville there were some really great teams. No bill was complete without one of these comedy acts: Willie and Eugene Howard, Clark and McCullough, Gallagher and Shean, Wheeler and Woolsey, Laurel and Hardy, Buck and Bubbles, Abbott and Costello, Van and Schenck, Olsen and Johnson, Healy and Cross—the greatest of these was Smith and Dale. Joe Smith is the only living member of this great family. He's ninety-two and living at the actors' home.

Actually, this was a tribute to Smith and Dale, who really were the Sunshine Boys. Joe couldn't miss this night. Walter and George were the first to rise to their feet when Joe Smith was introduced. Naturally, he was in his usual next to closing spot.

"I'm Doctor Kronkite's only living patient," he said. "Charlie Dale and I first joined the Friars in 1919. We used to do a little schtick— I'll have to do both parts, if I could remember it: 'Well, if it ain't my old friend Jake.' (Slaps him on the back very hard.)

" 'Hey, my name ain't Jake, and if it were Jake, is that any reason to slap me so hard on the back?'

" 'Well, if your name ain't Jake, then what do you care what I do to Jake?'

" 'By the way, where were you going when I stopped you?'

" 'I wasn't going. I was coming from the hospital, visiting my friend, Jacob P. Sonavitch.'

" 'Sonavitch? I loaned a sonavitch $25 once. Well, maybe that's another Sonavitch.' "

And that's how it went for fifteen minutes. The audience was screaming between tears. Walter, George, and all the comics on the dais laughed the loudest.

Again Smith and Dale stole the show. Joe said: "I just want to add a little ode to Charlie Dale. We've been together since 1898—over seventy years together. It's a great age we've lived in. From the horsecar to the jet planes. From Strauss to Irving Berlin. Over seventy years but it seems like yesterday from the old Atlantic Garden on the Bowery to the Palace on Broadway. We shared each other's sorrows, we shared each other's joys. In all phases of show business since we were a couple of boys. Over seventy years together. As close as two peas in a pod—and the only one that could separate us was God . . . thank you."

Even Neil Simon, the author of *The Sunshine Boys*, couldn't follow that—he just bowed and embraced Joe and the new Sunshine Boys—Burns and Matthau.

Walter Matthau said, "Vaudevillians are better actors. They have to be better because they are tempered by the storms of adversity and that is the only way to grow. Tonight I bow to my partner, ladies and gentlemen—you'll never see another man like George Burns again—so listen closely."

"I'd like to reminisce with you," George said. "To think that fifty-five years ago Jesse Block first saw me on the stage and said, 'George take my advice and get out of show business.' So I did. I teamed up with Billy Lorraine. We were on the bill with the Kromwell

Sisters. Very pretty girls that were contortionists. And I went around with Lilly Kromwell. And that girl could take both her legs and wrap them around her neck and she did some pretty good stuff on the stage, too.

"Well, as you all know, I'm now in a movie. I play Al Lewis, who's supposed to be old, comes from New York, and is Jewish. I don't know how I got the part. I'm old. I come from New York. I don't know how the hell they found out I was Jewish. Who knows, I might turn out to be a great character actor. Look, I might even be good enough to play a Gentile. If I played a Gentile, I'd have to play it from the waist up. If I played it from my waist down, I would have to use a lot of makeup. And I found it's much easier to play a character actor than it is to be a comedian, because a character actor doesn't have to get laughs. Come to think of it the last time I played Las Vegas I was a character actor.

"Anyway, I want to thank the Friars for having Walter and me here tonight. It's been beautiful. I'll always remember this night." Dean Buddy Howe gave them the Friars Oscar to help them remember, "and here it is another closing of another show."

It was more than just another show to a lot of us in that room. And it was the closing of a great era. It was a tribute to some of the beautiful clowns who brought so much joy into my life: the Marx Brothers, Fred Allen and Jack Benny, the Ritz Brothers. It was Joe Frisco and Eddie Davis, Ben Blue, Bert Lahr, and Charlie Chaplin. I was thinking of Harold Lloyd and Laurel and Hardy and Eddie Cantor, of Georgie Jessel and Richy Craig, Jr., and of Burns and Allen and Block and Sully, and the original Sunshine Boys, Smith and Dale, and an era that could never happen again.

PRAE OMNIA FRATERNITAS

Index